Martyrdom of Women

A Study of Death Psychology in the Early Christian Church to 301 CE

Arthur Frederick Ide

Garland
Tangelwüld
1985

Published by
Tangelwüld Press
P.O. Box 475961
Garland, Texas 75047-5961

©**1985, Arthur Frederick Ide**

Library of Congress Cataloging in Publication Data

Ide, Arthur Frederick.
   Martyrdom of women in the early Christian Church.

   Bibliography: p.
   Includes index.
   1. Martyrdom (Christianity)--Psychological aspects.
2. Women in Christianity--History--Early church,
ca. 30-600. I. Title.
BR1604.2.I33 1985   272'.1'088042   8514741
ISBN 0-934667-00-4 (pbk.)

**For
Hilton & Jo Anna Ratterree**

Table of Contents

ABBREVIATIONS

Allard, I. *HP*

Allard, Paul. *Histoire des Persecutions pendant les deux premiers Siecle* (Paris, 1892, 2d ed.)

CSEL

Corpus Scriptorum Ecclesiasticorum Latinorum (Vienna, in progress).

F. Conybeare *MEC*

Conybeare, F. *Monuments of Early Christianity* (London, 1894).

F. Cumont *TM*

Cumont, F. *Textes et Monuments figures relatifs aux mysteres de Mithra* (Bruxelles, 1899).

V. Duruy *HR*

Duruy, V. *Histoire des Romains* (Paris, 1871).

L. Duchesne *LP*

Duchesne, L. *Le Liber Pontificalis* (Paris, 1886; 2 vols.).

Gebhardt *AMS*

Gebhardt, Otto v. *Acta Martyrum Selecta* (Berlin, 1902).

A. Harnack *CAL*

_____. *The Expansion of Christianity in the First Three Centuries* (London, 1904; 2 vols.)

A. Harnack *MC*

_____. *Militia Christi* (Tubingen, 1907).

Lactantius *MP*

de Mortibus Persecutorum.

Lucian *PP*

Proteus Peregrinus.

Lightfoot *CLEM*	Lightfoot, Bp. *Clement* in *Apostolic Fathers* Pt. 1 (London, 1890; 2d ed., 2 vols).
Lightfoot *Ign.*	_____. *St. Ignatius and St. Polycarp in Apostolic Fathers.* (London, 1889; 2d ed., 3 vols).
Le Blant *SAM*	Le Blant, E. *Supplement aux Acta Martyrum Sincera* in *Memoires de Litterature* (Paris, 1881; vol. 30).
Le Blant *ICG*	_____. *Inscriptiones Christianos Galliae* (Paris, various dates)
Migne *PG*	Migne, J.-P. (ed.) *Patrologia cursus completus...serie Graeca* (Paris, various dates)
Migne *PL*	Migne, J.-P. (ed.) *Patrologia cursus completus ...serie Latina* (Paris, various dates)
Neumann *RSK*	Neumann, C.J. *Der Romische Staat und die allgemeine Kirche* (Leipzig, 1890f).
Ramsay *ChE*	Ramsay, W. *The Church in the Roman Empire* (London, 1894; 3rd ed.).
Ruinart *AM*	Ruinart, T. *Acta Martyrum Sincera* (Amsterdam, 1713; 2d ed.; also Ratisbon, 1893-).
ST	*Studi e Testi* (Rome, 1900-).
Tillemont	Le Nain de Tillemont. *Memoires pour servir a l'histoire ecclesiastique des six premiers sieles* (Venice, 1732; 15 vols.).

TU

Texte und Untersuchungen zur Geschichte der Altchristlichen Litteratur, ed. Otto von Gebhardt and Adolphe Harnack. Quoted by volume and year of publication.

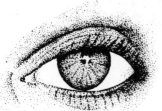

Martyrdom
of Women

Arthur Frederick Ide

The Psychology of Martyrdom

"Death holds no sting," early Christian martyrs reportedly declared as they marched or were led away to their deaths, according to the parchment writings of early hagiographers. Death by martyrdom neither was feared nor avoided by the early Christian community. Instead many zealous neophytes rushed into the arms of death, to be "embraced in that sweetness of the bridegroom who awaits" in anticipation of "journeying on to a better place, to a mansion which has many rooms, where there is no pain, nor hunger, nor thirst, but only constant rejoicing." "It is a reward, a fulfilling of life's destiny to die for the Lord Jesus Christ," came the cry of those who watched the beasts, gladiators, and other means of mortal dispatch bear down upon them, for such an act was consciously considered the highest expression of ultimate love and devotion to God.[1]

Not only was physical martyrdom openly sought, but many of the most confirmed Christians argued for the "privilege of surrendering this existence for immortal life. Their attitude was a simple statement that life on earth had no mean-

[1]There are numerous records on the acts of the martyrs, the most favored being the *Acta Sanctorum.* The Bollandist Society, as well as numerous other societies have also issued tracts of the alleged martyrological records. As for the secular view, see Hadrian's letter to Servianus, as preserved by Vopiscus, *Vita Saturnini* 8—although this letter's authenticity is questioned by some, such as T. Mommsen, *Provinces of the Roman Empire* (London, 1886, 2 vols.) II:227n., while it is accepted by others, such as V. Duruy, *Histoire des Romains* (Paris, 1871; English translation by P. Mahaffy, London, 1885; 6 vols.) V:94.

ing or purpose. Happily (it is recorded), with many singing and clapping their hands in joyous expectation, the early Christian martyrs walked—and even danced—into what was considered "the darkness of death," eager "to see by eternal light" "the source of their love, their lover and bridegroom." The "chosen ones who have sacrified their flesh for a robe of purity" were applauded by their co-religionists "who had not yet been crowned with the laurel of immortality"and even by some "of them who are still of this world" who did not accept the Christian *credo*. "Still the witnessing of those who are about to see the Christ, like those who are with the Crucified, brings new souls to the testimony and baptism of faith." The non-Christians saw in the Christians who accepted martyrdom at the hand of the state a special and unique strength, a confession of loyalty that had lapsed among the masses.[2] Their conversations led others to inquries concerning the strange and dissettling faith from the orient, and about its teacher, a simple carpenter from Galilee who had been tried and executed as a common criminal in the most cruel manner the empire knew at that time—by being nailed to a cross like any common thief.[2] At the same time, those who were called upon to demonstrate the intensity of their religious convictions, to accept the crown of martyrdom, were strengthened by [3]

[2]Clement of Alexandria, *Stromata* IV:4; Tertullian, *Ad Martyrium* 3.

[3]Lucian, *Proteus Peregrinus* (ed. Dindorf) III:337. Cf. Tertullian, *Apologia* 40, and Cyprian, *Ad Demetrius* 2. Eusebius, *Historia Ecclesia* IV:13, carries it into a discussion.

the various ministrations "of those who continued to endure this existence in hopes that they, too, will be called to real life." Those who "remained behind" and "suffered in the flesh" were known as "confessors"—many of whom were articulate and literate. These "confessors" spent numerous hours in hiding—frequently in the darkened confines of a closet or shed—writing on the *passiones* (the court records of the trials, judgments, and executions, which cannot, in themselves, be considered totally reliable and authentic, as the purpose of the *passiones* was not to leave a genuine record of the events leading up to and completing the execution, but rather to "teach and instruct the faithful") of the martyrs, glorifying their death as not only being "righteous" but "a source for others to take spirit." One such "confessor" declared, "*Blessed martyrs, you who have been tried by fire like fine gold, you are now crowned with the diadem that cannot fade away; for you have bruised beneath your feet the serpent's* [Satan] *head*"[4]—thus giving the martyrs a recognition of being equal to Jesus Christ. Even Tertullian (Quintus Septimius Florens Tertullianus, born in Carthage, North Africa, approximately 160 CE, and died around the year 230 CE, a Christian for a part of his life, who is still considered a Latin Father of the Church on

[4]T. Ruinart, *Acta Martyrum Sincera* (2d ed.; Amsterdam, 1713), 222. The various *passiones* compiled by later scholars have not yet been completely translated into contemporary languages, although a sizeable number are to be found in such works published in the ancient languages of Latin, Greek, and Arabic, as given by J.-P. Migne, in the multivolume work *Patrologia ... cursus completus.*

the basis of his writings—the vast majority of which are decidely and boldly anti-women) wrote that the pain and suffering experienced by the Christians who were "martyred either in the flesh or the spirit" on "account of their faith" had willingly paid the price to merit "the crown of eternity itself.[5] It was this *signo vinces* of faith and the ultimate demonstration of love as testified in the final testimony of "laying down ones life so that the faith can live,"[6] that encouraged countless numbers of men and women to "reach for the laurel of holy martyrdom."

Dying for the faith of Jesus Christ was considered by the majority of early Christians, the single most important means of demonstrating their passion and zeal of the faith. Dying for the faith, in fact, meant more to the early Christians than living in this world—even if the life "on this earth is spent in open witnessing by water [baptism] and the word [preaching]."

Only a few of those who had suffered in the mines and quarries of the Roman Empire—being bannished to select islands and territorial work-areas, could be (or were) considered "true martyrs"—without having to die for that particular distinction. The "living testimony" of these men and women was considered to be a witness to the teachings of Jesus—but not on par with the actual "laying down of one's life." Still their testimony was heralded and widely acclaimed—their example and endurance of pain elevated to a

[5]Tertullian, *loc. cit.*

[6]John 17:1. Cf. Tertullian, *Apologia* 37.

near canonized stature, as defined by Church Fathers who relied on exegesis of scripture.[7] Some theologians even argued that there was a special mark of martyrdom if the victim was accused of being a "crucified Sophist,"[8] since such an appellation had the distinction (it was argued) of actually being "a glory"[9] since no other god had had such an end earthly end, nor had any other god accepted or expected equal immitation from any follower and believer.[10]

Those dedicated Christians, who willingly "dedicated themselves to following in all ways the manner and life and teachings of our Lord Jesus Christ," not only won the lauds of co-religionists, but also merited remission of sins both venial and mortal: a concept slowly emerging in western Christianity by the end of the second century CE. These "marks of merit" primarily permitted penitent believers to atone for the "sins" or infractions made in the past—before they accepted the teachings of the followers of Christ, although in time this "Treasury of Merit" would be expanded to include sins committed during their life as a Christian, and, by the fifteenth and sixteenth centuries, for sins committed after contrition, shrevement, and penance: both for the sins of ommission and commission (the concept of "sin" and the penalties for sin had

---

[7]Eusebius, *op. cit.*, VIII:11.

[8]Phil. 2:7.

[9]Lucian, *op. cit.*, III:330.

[10]Justin, *Apologia*, I:55.

not yet been introduced or given the *ex cathedra* seal of the church. Instead, the entire penitential system would wait for a thousand years before it would be refined and systematized). Such as system of atonement was graphically laid out in Justin's *Apology*:[11]

> There was a woman maried to a man who lived an evil life—[a life] *in which she, too, had previously taken part. But once she had come to know the teachings of Christ, she reformed, and tried to persuade her husband to reform his own life as well, calling to his mind the doctrine of Christ and warning him of the eternal fire prepared for those who did not live according to discipline and the right way of knowledge. But the man persisted in his licentiousness, and alienated his wife by his actions. His wife then thought that it would be wrong to continue to live with the man who sought his pleasures from any source whatsoever, no matter whether that pleasure was against justice or the natural law—and so she sought a divorce from him. Her relatives, however, earnestly entreated her to remain with him on the ground that her husband might one day attain the hope of changing his life; and so she forced herself to stay with him.*[12]

She later left her husband when he would not reform. <u>Afterwards she was martyred by the state.</u>

[11]Justin, *Apologia* II.2; *Corpus apologetarum christianorum*; ed. C. Otto (Jena, 1879) III:266f.

[12]Eusebius, *op. cit.*, IV:17

Early Christians believed that personal faith in a deity (which was translated as being personified (*persona*) in the form and nature of a man known as Jesus of Nazareth) was more important than anything else. For this faith many early Christians were unquestionably willing to sacrifice everything: home, family, spouse, protection, food, shelter, even life. 73% of those who chose to suffer some form of personal or familial deprivation were women (based on a statistical analysis of existing *passiones* and other extant documents of this era). And even though Jesus had allegedly spoken out against divorce and condemned it, the early Christians accepted separation from a spouse who would not convert to the message of the Nazarene, and lived as if they were divorced. Once divorce was granted by the state a sizeable number of the new sectarians remarried even though the spouse was alive—- quite in common with the general consensus of the time. There is no record of any Christian contesting the divorce proceedings, nor objecting to the action and ruling of the court in divorce matters. Instead there are records of the acquiesence to the ruling. After the divorce decree some did not remarry. The majority of those who did not remarry (70%) were women. They entered the service of the church as a "deacon" to minister by faith and deed).

"Standing fast, foot to foot in the fight for Christ" was translated as being willing to defend the message of Jesus against all odds. To do so would bring to the adherent the title and dignity of being a living witness—or *martyr*. Fighting was not meant to be a retaliatory confrontation generating violence, bloodshed, or loss of life— but the intent was not always the reality and practice. It was only the intent.

The intent of the martyrs exist in select records maintained and preserved by the ancient church and its subsequent development. These records exist today because concerned Christians believed that not only were the testimonies of the martyrs and their subsequent *passiones* (or death records) significant for their own time, but would be a source of inspiration for future generations which might experience persecution because of their faith. Thus concerned Christians in the early days of the church, as late as 310, delighted in deligently preserving the records at all costs during the times of persecution, and even during times when the state permitted the confessors of Christ relative freedom—even if the persevrance of the records in, and of, and by themselves became tantamount to sealing one's own death warrant: *in lupanari nudam statui praecipio.*[13] This was especially true in the early years of the fourth century, when many martyrs, especially as testified in the records of the trials of the holy women Agape and Chione, detail.

Most of the commentaries on the execution of the martyrs—especially the accounts of the women who gave up their lives voluntarily in testimony to their religious faith in the deity of Jesus and of his relationship to the Father, argue that the cases that were presented to the state in

[13]See Appendix A.

quest of taking their lives was *ipso facto* based on their being Christians and their public ministrations in witnessing the birth, life, message, and death of Jesus of Nazareth.[14] This *apologia* continued for centuries—even down to the twentieth where historians and theologians continue to argue that early Christians suffered primarily for their religious convictions and pronouncements.[15] However, even though the evidence does point to a reality and worthiness of this argument in part, it cannot be considered or accepted as certainly, universally, and solidly infallible as it is argued. This is because these arguments which give a quasihaliographic definition of martyrdom (or witnessing), do not take into consideration the emotions, psychology (overt and/or covert), and the needs, interpretations, fears and expectations of the state—viewing all as a composite whole rather than isolated incidents. Nor do these arguments consider the individuals who were martyred as individuals; nor, too, do these arguments consider the humanity, psychology and patriotism of the judges, accusers, and executioners before and after the death of the chronicled martyrs—some of whom, in fact, became Christian because of the martyrdoms: before, during, or after the actual assundering of the confessor's mortal existence.

[14]Clement of Rome, *Cor.* 5.

[15]Cf. H.B. Workman, *Persecution in the Early Church* (London, 1923), *passim*.

[16]Cf. A.N. Sherwin-White, "The Early Persecutions and Roman Law Again," *JTS* n.s. 3 (1952), pp. 208ff.

The one-time church Father Tertullian argued that the general laws were *adversus Christianos*, but such a claim is only partially correct. The laws which Tertullian cites are laws for all of the empire and all of the citizens of the empire. These laws were (as close as possible) equally enforced on followers of any deity whose precepts forbade the faithful from serving in the Roman army, or fulfilling the basic and specific requirements demanded of patriotic citizens. Thus it is far more accurate to view the persecutions in the light that the Christian community constituted *collegia illicita*—a reality many enjoyed, experienced and flaunted because it was different (to startling) than the mainstream interpretation of what human existence required as a means of acceptable expression—and therefore they placed themselves into the position of becoming subject to the enforcement of the *lex Iulia de collegiis*..[17] The early Christians, by comparison, were "odd balls" who delighted in eccentricities which shocked their fellow citizens—very much in the same manner as twentieth century "hippies" or "punk rockers" tantilize their contemporaries by outlandish appearances and life styles. And, as the twentieth century CE is as intolerant of differences within its scope, so too, the Roman empire at the time of the martyrdoms was intolerant of that which was uncommon.

It was on the grounds of the early Christians eccentricities that many of the initial charges were brought before magistrates within the Roman em-

[17]Cf. Tertullian, *Apologia*, XXXIX, 14-21, ed. E. Dekkers, p. 152. 60-100.

pire. It was on this basis, almost exclusively, that the emperors and their legal representatives throughout the empire operated, for Rome realized that a commonwealth could not exist without *pax et ordo* narrowly defined along traditional lines. It was the narrow definition of society and its laws that the early Christian community refused to adhere to since such adherence appeared to be "not according to the right way to live in the fear of Jesus Christ."[18] Early Christians were strongly opposed to the concept of "Live and let live," and wished to expunge themselves from any

---

[18]Sherwin-White, *op. cit.*., pp. 203-204. G.E.M. Ste. Croix, "Why Were the Early Christians Persecuted," *PP* 26 (1963), pp. 6-38. H. Last, "The Study of the Persecutions," *Journal of Roman Studies* 27 (1937) pp. 80ff. The articles are contemporary disagreements with traditionalists, such as Adolphe Harnack, who suggested that the Acts of the Christian martyrs were ultimately to be conceived as a continuation of the apostolic witnessing of and to the New Testament (see, A. Harnack, "Das ursprungliche Motiv der Abfassung von Maertyrer- und Heilungsacten in der Kirche," *Sitzungsb. koen. preuss. Akad. der Wiss* (1910), pp. 106-125) without regard for the actual literary problems. The best criticism of this oversight-to-error in ignoring the literary problems is Delehaye's *Les Passions des martyrs et les genres litteraires* (Bruxelles, 1921) which lays down practical criteria for distinguishing between historical and fictional *acta*. Some of the *passiones* are given in their entirety with a parallel translation into English from the original language, in my *Woman in the Age of Christian martyrs* (1980), or the two publications by Eastfield College, my translations of the passions of saints Crispina of Africa, and Agape, Irene, and Chione of Thessalonika (both, 1979). See also my (1975) *Collections of the Records of the Martyrdoms of Women in the Third Century*, and my (1974) *Collections of the Records of Martyrdoms of Women Persecuted in the First Two Hundred Years of the Early Christian Church.*

form of worldliness or difference that was around them, very much in the manner in which Jerry Falwell and the Moral Majority Political Action Committee in Twentieth Century America attempt to redefine American civilization and lifestyle along their narrow interpretations of what is correct.

Yet, when a lesser power attempts to dictate to a stronger power conflict arises that ends in the persecution of the lesser power. This lot befell the early Christians.

The Martyrdom of St. Juliet
From the altar front of SS. Quirce and Julita, Durro, Spain

Rome's Argument
Against the Christians

Christianity's first three hundred years within the Roman empire were filled with tragedy on all levels. Most of the tragedies experienced by the early Christians were group and individually induced, for, initially, Roman citizens had little animosity or hatred those who professed Christianity.

The majority of the Roman people saw the early Christians as simple atheists (*a-theos*). Early Christians were viewed as "atheists" since they followed the "irrational teachings of a mortal man who his followers claimed to be immortal, yet a god who died like a common mortal criminal, being nailed to a board and hung by an executioner for all to see." Jesus, Romans concluded, was only a "crucified Sophist."[19]

Charges of atheism leveled against Christians developed when Christians would not sacrifice for the good of the state, for peace, for prosperity, nor would they pray for the wisdom and justice for civil leaders. This seemed to say that the early Christians did not believe in a universal god who would guide and protect all people, insure a just government, and desire peace. The Christian god was seen as not a god but a petty local and isolated demigogue. Subsequently, Christians were viewed as atheists ("without god").

Since Christians did not pray for the peace and

[19]Lucian, *loc. cit.*

prosperity of the state (since most believed that the state was in "impious hands," worshipped false gods" and "was venial and corrupt,") and called the established gods (those who were common and everywhere accepted throughout the empire, such as Venus, Diana, Zeus, Mars, etc.) "demon gods": *Ego Christiana sum et numquam sacrificaui, daemoniis, nisi soli deo...*[20] which many equated with the men who "fashioned the images of the gods" in contradiction to the injunction of the Torah which forbade graven images, they were seen as a threat to law and order, peace and harmony—and, too, prosperity.

Early Christian hostility to the established gods and political life of the empire provoked violent anger among a traditionally tolerant people, for many Romans, leaders and civilians in all walks of life and stations of comfort, saw their deities as the only true gods who welcomed heartily any new gods into a pantheon confraternity that was equal to any melting-pot "where all can become as one."[21]

It was exceedingly difficult for the Roman citizenry who were not Christians to understand

[20]*Idus Aprilis sanctorum martyrum Carpi episcopi et Pamfili diaconi et Agathonicae*, codex latinus 4 of the Library of Bergamo (s. xi).

[21]O. von Gebhardt, "Das Martyrium des heiligen Pionius," *Archiv fur slavische Philologie* 18. 1-2 (1896) pp. 156-171: "we do not worship your so-called gods, nor willwe adore the golden idol [cf. Daniel 3:18]," IV. 15; and, *ibid.*, VIII.15: "I am a Christian," said Pionius, "I do not offer sacrifice to men." The Proconsul replied, "Surely it was the god, that is Zeus, who is in heaven; for he is the ruler of all of the gods." and *ibid.*, XIX.13.

the overt obstinancy and apparent atheism which led Christians into rejecting established, traditional gods—and ultimately lead to their own suffering and execution.

The Proconsul Anullinus declared:[22]

Are you aware of what is commanded by the sacred decree? To which Crispina responded: No, I do not know what has been ordered. Anullinus told her: That you should offer sacrifice to all of our gods for the welfare of the emperors, in accordance with the law issued by our lords the reverend Augusti Diocletian and Maximan and the most noble Caesars Constantius and Maximus. Crispina replied: I have never sacrificed and I shall not do so except to the one true God and to our Lord Jesus Christ, his son, who was born and did die. Anullinus, the Proconsul said, Break with this superstition and bow your head to the sacred rites of the gods of Rome. Crispina replied:

Praecepti sacri cognouisti sententiam? Crispina respondit: Quid praeceptum sit nescio. Anullinus dixit: Ut Omnibus diis nostris pro salute principum sacrifices, secundum legem datam a dominis nostris Diocletiano et Maximiano piis Augustis et Constantio et et Maximo nobilissimis Caesaribus. Crispina respondit: Numquam sacrificaui nex sacrifico nis uni et uero Deo et domino nostro Iesu Christo filio eius, qui natus et passus est. Anullinus proconsul dixit: Amputa supersititionem et subiuga caput tuum ad sacra deorum Romanorum. Crispina respondit: Cotidie

---

[22]Text in P. Franchi de Cavalieri, "Nuove note agiografichi: ii. Osservazioni sopra gli Atti di s. Crispina," *ST* 9 (1902) pp. 32-35: I-6. A complete text and translation is found in my *Woman in the Age of Christian martyrs*, Appendix II, with translation and commentary in my *The Martyrdom of the Lady Crispina* (1979).

Statue of Isis (above) was a common art theme in the ancient Roman world. Though originally Egyptian in origin, Isis became a Greek goddess during the Hellenistic age. Her cult spread throughout the civilized world which profoundly affected and influenced the Christian cult of Mary, the Mother of Jesus, who many believed she was. From the Mansell Collection [Brogi] at the Museo Nazionale in Naples.

Every day I worship my God Almighty. I know of no other God besides him. Anullinus said: You are a stubborn and isolent woman and you will soon feel the force of our laws against your will. Crispina replied: Whatever happens I shall be glad to suffer it on testimony to the faith I hold. Anullinus said: It is mere folly in your mind that you will not put aside this superstition and worship the sacred gods.

adoro Deum meum omnipotentem: praeter eum nullum alium Deum noui. Anullinus dixit: Dura es et contemptrix, et incipies uim legum inuita sustinere. Crispina respondit: Quicquid emerserit, pro fide mea quam teneo, libenter patior. Anullinus dixit: Vanitas est animi tui ut non iam dimissa supersititione sacra numina uenereris.

The charge of atheism fell most heavily on women. Traditionally women were expected to tend the sacred gardens and care for the temples of the Olympian deities who they worshipped and adored. The temples could be either civic edifices, or simple wayside chapels and altars. The old gods were seen as protectors of the house, the road, fields, the treasury, pantry, and society in general. Select deities had dominions over the common cold, headaches, soar throats, fevers, lost articles, forests, rain, fertility, agriculture, purity, wisdom, piety, vocations, occupations, and the like—all of which would later be incorported into the Christian worship in the same manner as the cult of Isis became the Christian cult of St. Mary the mother of Jesus.

Much of the early theology of the deities of Rome were generated in prehistoric records of motherhood. These markings of motherhood of the gods of Rome were transferred to the Christian god: *Numquam sacrificaui nex sacrifico nisi uni et uero Deo et domino nostro Iesu Christo filio eius, qui natus et passus est. ... Cotidie ueneror, sed Deum uium et uerum, qui est dominus meus, praeter quem alium non noui.*[23]

So zealous was the will of the Christian confessor-women that the majority of those of whom we have records eagerly went to their deaths in a revivalistic willingness equal to the ancient sacrifices of virgins to the gods of fire and the sun.[24] Their intent and purpose was identical: they saw in their deaths the glorification of their deity, the defense of the deity, and the spiritual cleansing of their bodies and souls from earthly corruption so that they "might gain and hold eternal life."

Christian zeal to seek out martyrdom to please the Christian god was interpreted by the ancient Romans to be a disgusting re-enactment of primitive blood worship. But it, at the same time, was excused as sport—similar to that which was watched with joyous excitation in the arenas built throughout the expanding empire.

The zeal of Christian women in seeking out and accepting martyrdom was especially depressing and revolting to Roman citizens. Letters were written denouncing such situations where women "threw away their lives in eager anticipation of winning the crown of death—which they equate with the 'Crown of Immortal Life'.":

[23]*Ibid.* Note the reply of Crispina: "I worship daily. But I worship the living and true god who is my Lord—and beside him I recognize no others."

[24]Text is in Eusebius, *EH* V.1.3-2.8, especially I:17

All the wrath of the mob, the Prefect *and the soldiers fell with an overwhelming furry on the deacon Sanctus of Vienne; on Maturus who was, though newly baptized, a noble athlete, on Attalus whose family had migrated from Pergamum, who had always been a pillar and ground of the community there; and, on Blandina, through whom Christ proved that the things that men think cheap, ugly, and contemptuous are deemed worthy of glory before God, by reason of her love for Him which was not merely vaunted in appearance but demonstrated in achievement.*

All of us were in terror; and Blandina's earthly mistress who was herself among the martyrs in the conflict, was in agony lest because of her bodily weakness she would not be able to make a bold confession of her faith. Yet, Blandina was filled with such a fortitude that even those who were taking turns to torture her in every way from sun-up to sunset were weary and exhausted; they themselves admitted that they were beaten, that there was nothing further that they could do to cause her pain, and that they were surprised that she was still breathing—for her entire body was torn and broken. They testified that every kind of torture was sufficient to release her soul, let alone the many that they applied with such strength. Instead, this blessed woman, like a noble athlete was granted new strength with her confession of faith: her testimonial that, "I am a Christian; we do nothing to be ashamed of," brought her refreshment, rest, and an insensibility to her present pain.''[25]

The Christians' insistence on signing hymns at the time of their execution was even more confusing to the ancient Romans. The melody of psalms and prayers that rose from the throats of those who were about to be dispatched from this earthly existence brought the crowds in the arenas to a furious roar, crying out for their immediate deaths with no mercy to be shown, while those who approached their doom believed fervently that they were about to embark on a journey towards peace and bounty:

Perpetua then began to sing a hymn: she was already treading on the head of the Egyptian. Revocatus, Saturninus, and Saturus began to warn the watching mob. Then when they came within the sight of Hilarianus they suggested by their motions and gestures: "You have condemned us, but god will condemn you;" that is what they were suggesting by their motions and gestures. At this the crowds became enraged and demanded that they be scourged before a line of gladiators. And the rejoiced at this that they had ob-

Perpetua psallebat caput iam Aegyptii calcans. Reucatus et Saturninus et Saturus populo spectanti comminabantur, dehinc ut sub conspectu Hilariani peruenerunt, gestu et nutu coperunt Hilariano dicere: "Tu nos, inquiunt, te autem Deus," ad hoc populus exasperatus flagellis eos uexari per ordinem uenatorum postulauit; et utique gratulati sunt quod aliquid

[25]*Ibid.* 17-19.

tained a share in the Lord's suffering."   et dominicis passionibus essent consecuti.[26]

Unlike previous martyrdoms, the martyrs in this account goaded, chided, belittled and insulted the crowds until the populace demanded their death. The martyrs in this case cannot be excused nor can their end be justified as a quiet testimony of faith and a heading towards union with a deity. Instead, at a deeper reading of the text, especially the line *gestu et nutu coperunt*, one must conclude that the eagerness for martyrdom was so strong that all senses and intents of charity (*caritatis*) were missing in the people who were dispatched that time. Although the persecution and liquidation of a person who holds a differing opinion can never be excused, pardoned, or forgiven, it must still be acknowledged that the persecution reached its zenith in this situation only when those who were condemned urged the expediency of the executor to carry out their sentences. In part such a situation does qualify as suicide since it is the deliberate working towards one's own death. This account, therefore, is a record of mass hysteria leading to mass suicide—not to religious martyrdom.

Yet, within the same account there is a marked and singular presentation of true martyrdom.

[26]C.J.M.J. van Beek, *Passio sanctarum Perpetuae et Felicitatis* (Nijmegen, 1936) pp. 1-62. van Beek has combined nine manuscripts of the Latin recension in his critical edition, bringing the text in line with that of Tertullian. The exact passage reads, "Perpetua then began to sing a hymn" showing that her psalmatry was a result of the introduction of the act of persecution and not a goading towards assuring the execution of herself and her co-religionists.

While the majority of those who died were suicides—with the greatest number of those in that dispatchment being men—it is also clear from the same account that some few did qualify as persecuted people and martyrs who attempted until the final moment to perserve their life and even to help settle the unrest. In these cases it was women, not men, who stood forth to reason and disuade, as in the case of the Martyr Perpetua:[27]

The military tribune had treated them with extraordinary harshness because he was given information by certain people which made him afraid that they [the Christians] would be lifted out of prison through magic. Perpetua spoke to him directly: "Why can't you even permit us to refresh outselves properly? For we are the most distinguished of the condemned prisoners as we belong to the emperor: we are to fight on his birthday. Would it not be to your credit if we were brought out on that day in a healthier condition?

...cum tribunus castigatius eos castigaret, quia ex admonitionibus hominum uanissimorum uerebatur ne subtraherentur de carcere incantationibus aliquibus magicis, in faciem ei Perpetua respondit: Quid utique non permittis nobis refrigerare noxiis nobilissimis, Caesaris scilicet, et natali eiusdem pugnaturis? aut non tua gloria est, si pinguiores illo producamur?

The fear held by the Tribunes had some justification. What added additional credulity to the rumors that the Christians were plotting to

27*Ibid.*, 16.

escape from the prisons and their sentences of death was the fact that many of the condemned not only laughed at the reading of the sentence, but vowed that they would live long after their tormentors had perished. The charge of insanity was commonly attached to the persecuted Christians as well, for many of those who laughed at the reading of their death warrants, also laughed and ridiculed their executioners as they were being led to the place of their dispatchment, as occured with the young woman Sabrina:[28]

[After being read her death warrant] Sabrina smiled at this and at the verger and his men who said, "You laugh?"

"If God so wills, I do. You see, we are Christians. Those who believe in Christ will laugh unhesitatingly in everlasting joy," she replied.

They told her: "You are going to suffer something you do not like: women who refuse to sacrifice are put into a brothel." She replied to this, "The god who is holy will take care of this."

···μειδιωσης δε της Σαβινης ο νεωκορος και οι μετ᾽ αυτου ειπον Γελας η δε ειπεν Ἐαν ο ϑελη ναι· Χριστιανοι γαρ εις Χριστον πιστευουσιν αδιστακτως γελασουσιν εν χαρα αιδιω λεγουσιν αυτη Ευ μεν ο ου ϑελεις μελλεις πασχειν, αι γαρ μη επιϑυουσαι εις πορνειον ισταντα᾽ι η δε ειπεν, Τω αγιω ϑεω μελησει περι τουτου.

---

[28]Full text and translation in my *Execution of the Lady Sabrina* (1977). Also see my *Woman in the Age of Christian martyrs*, p. 15 and note.

Since many Christian women refused to give up "their countenance" it became standard for Proconsuls and Perfects to "tempt away" the Christian by either offering sex or by forcing the Christian into participating in sex against her will. The belief was then, like it has been throughout generations, that a woman will accept the dictates of man once she experiences sex. In part the Christian apologists adversion to denial of sex and sexuality developed from the need to make sex distasteful—or "something to be endured, offering it up to the Lord as a penance, a cross of one's own to carry in this world of sin." Romans, on the other hand, did not see sex in the same light, but accepted it as a natural occurance—provided, of course that the act was heterosexual, and the technique was penial intromission. Homosexuality was as little tolerated in the Roman empire as it was in the early Christian community. Homosexuality, however, was not damned as being sinful, according to Roman writers, but because it was an act "best left alone for the satisfaction of the gods," and because it would cost the state the necessary manpower to defend itself with—either in denying the conception and birth of new soldiers, or by (supposedly) weakening the fighting resolve of the military. Thus, when there were suspected cases of overt homosexuality within the community, the "most effective way to arrest" it was by having the alleged homosexual copulate with a member of the opposite sex (castration or execution was reserved for those who failed to "change"). This is significant and important to understand, for several of the Roman jurists suspected Christian Virgins (women who either took a vow of chastity and celibacy, or were widows and refused to remarry) of being lesbians. Thus the alleged female homosexual was to be "converted by the joy of a man's instrument."

To avoid sexual intercourse when placed in a brothel, many early Christian women committed suicide. Others attempted to (and a few succeeded) run away—usually into the hills. Such activities increased Roman fears of a massive Christian exodus—similar to that taken by the Jews in the days of Rameses II. But even greater than was the fear of Christians escaping was the Roman fear of Christians proselytizing. This uneasiness of Christians missionarizing among the non-Christians was very real, especially with the increase of the number of Christians who were ordained to the priesthood: as deacons, ministers, and bishops. A sizeable number of those ordained were women,[29] who were especially effective in winning the allegiance and conversion of the aged, the young, women, and minorities, not only among the social outcasts, but even within the imperial circle.

Both to stop the suspected exodus, and to curb the proselytization of the Christians, Rome

---

[29]*PG* I, cols. 1115-1118, *Apostolic Constitutions* Book 1, chaps. 19-20. Cp. my *Woman in early Christianity and Christian society* (1980) pp. 5f, my *Teaching of Jesus on Women* (1984), and my *Woman as Priest, Bishop and Laity in the Early Catholic Church, with a complete and parallel translation of Romans 16 and other patrological writings on the role of women in the early Christian community to 440 AD.* (1984).

enacted legislation prohibiting Christians to travel.[30] The missionary zeal of women increased, however, with the enforcement of the law—for many women saw the law as unjust and openly vowed to defy it, giving as the excuse for their civil disobedience that "god's law is higher than is the law of man."

Early Christian women augmented their missionary activities of teaching and preaching, with collecting, compiling, and sometimes transcribing and even writing books, letters, monograms, and other hortatory works. The purpose was twofold: one, it preserved the teachings and laws of the Apostles which were not contained in letters allegedly written by the Apostles, and two, because a learned individual was held in respect and the scholar's word accepted and obeyed with little question.[32] Women who could write were especially feared, "for they have mastered a sacred art, one reserved for the gods and for men," and thus "became like the gods on the same footing as men."[33]

---

[30]See my *Execution of the Holy Women Snow, Peace and Love at Thessalonika* (1979).

[31]*Ibid.*, especially the line "A man named Terentius shouted out from the crowd: 'Do you know that this fellow has aroused up others so as not to sacrifice [to the established and recognized gods]?' " *loc. cit.*

[32]"Do you have in your possession any writings, parchments, or books of the impious Christians," asked the Perfect. *Ibid.*

[33]*Ibid.*

Many of the writings of the early church authors, especially those by and of women, placed harsh and self-sacrificing restrictions on individual lifestyles of adherents and neophytes (those who wished to become a part of the Christian community and underwent cathecatical instruction, baptism, and congregational introduction). Not only were limitations placed upon the early Christians by their religious leaders, many of whom were women, but previously experienced "freedoms"—especially in the matter of individual choices which were traditionally bestowed upon the individual by the city (*civitas omnium numinum cultrix*[34])—were done away with entirely. Those who accepted the message of Jesus as expressed and preached by those who claimed to follow him and were ordained by him, did not object to the forfeiture of these freedoms and liberties, but voluntarily surrendered them—sometimes *en masse*. In giving up their individualities and individual and personal freedoms, these early Christians confessed that they accepted the word of the priests of Jesus and believed fervently that they would receive a greater and more lasting freedom "in the bosom of Jesus." These rewards were to be "forever—from this day forward into the world that never ends—a paradise of great beauty and comfort with much singing and rejoicing in the Lord."[35] This idea, although not

---

[34]Arnobius, *Adv. Gent.* VI.7.

[35]Ruinart, *AM* 550. Harnack, *MC* 119-121, and his comments in *CAL* II:477n. Cp. John XVIII:38, and Acts XXVI:28.

anathema to the Romans, was definitely not understood and appeared on reflection to be incomprehensible.

To possess any of these writings, especially those that discussed "another world" and the "King who reigns there—world without end" was considered a capital crime since there was to be only one king of Rome, and Rome, it was commonly believed, would be the kingdom without end. To say or write otherwise was treason, and to be found guilty of treason would bring about the death penalty both to the writer of such words and ideas, and too to the possessor and reader of such words for censorship was strong and necessary in a totalitarian nation which required a oneness to complete and compliment its cosmopolitan commonweal. The Christian writings were adverse to this union of church and state as existed with the pantheon of gods and the empire, and wrote violently against such an existence and state of affairs, giving even more reason to the state officials to fear them and consider the Christians to be social deviants whose deviance had to be controlled at all costs.[36]

---

[36]This was difficult for Roman society in general to understand, for many of the Christian tenents of faith were identical or closely similar to those of other world faiths. This was especially true with the cult of Isis which gave Christianity much of its ideas and rites on the veneration of Mary, the mother of Jesus.

The concept of a saviour was a part of both the stories of the life of Jesus and of Aesculapius; even Isis and Mithra were viewed a saviours. All of these individuals brought the dead back to life,, all promised those who believed in them and followed their teachings immortal life in a paradise.

The paradises—or great parks—were universally the

same, as was the concept of their being an "elect number" of those who would obtain "eternal life." The rituals to be exercised, the prayers which were to be said, and the sacrifices of all the faiths were in common with one another. Objectively, there was little difference in any of the faiths of Rome, even though each claimed that it was unique and different, the "only road (or way) to salvation," through its god or goddess who was divinely begotten, suffered and did die for the evils, sins, and transgressions of the mortal race. See Harnack, *EC.* I, c. 2, especially i, 146, n.; and, Ramsay, *CBP* I:52, 104, 138, 262-264, 348. For Mithra and the cult of Mithraism—Christianity's strongest and most zealous rival which nearly conquered the faith—see F. Cumont, *Textes et Monuments figures relatifs aux mysteres de Mithra* (Bruxelles, 1899). On Isis, see Dill, *RSNA*, 560-585, and the exhaustive expose in Lafaye, *Histoire du Culte des Divinites d'Alexandrie hors de l'Egypte* (Paris, 1884).

The male head of the family, the *paterfamilias*, had absolute control of its members in the early days of Rome, but by the imperial age this had become for all intents and purposes fiction. Under the Caesars, Roman women, particularly of the upper classes, were free to pursue their own interests, acquire an education, manage their own property, divorce and remarry, intervene in politics—aspects which were dissettling to the early Christians by the third century CE who believed that women should be subject to the man, remain in the house, and speak only when spoken to. Above, courtesy of the Metropolitan Museum of Arts, Rogers Fund (1903) shows a woman playing the cithera, an ancient form of the lute.

Christian Limits on Freedom

Sex was a primary concern of early Christians, and was to be strictly regulated if it was not voluntarily eschewed, abstained from, or made impossible to experience by disfiguring or desexing oneself. Regulation of human sexuality was accomplished primarily by requiring any adherent to abstain from any form of sex, including masturbation, until s/he was married. Then, after marriage, sex was to be coital and engaged in only for the purpose of procreation.

Abstinence, celibate apologists argued, was the highest form of godliness. God, allegedly, did not have to have sex in human form to create, and thus sex was more a manifestation of human weakness than of godly strength. To honor god, it was held, humankind ought to attempt to imitate the deity in every way, the easiest being to abandon any and all sexual interests and expressions.

To dissuade neophytes and practioners of the Christian cult, a series of regulations and restrictions were placed on human sexuality. Foremost among these codes of conduct was the requirement that sex take place only after a religious marriage had been contracted, vows exchanged before a priest, and a commitment made to "be fruitful and multiply." This fruition would be realized in coital intercourse between husband and wife (male-female), and then only at the time of possible ovulation and impregnation. Although later generations have argued that the technique was limited to a strict horizontal position (sometimes called the "missionary position"), there is no foundation in fact of record for such a claim. However, "licentiousness" was broadly defined to include any form of "promiscuity" which was defined as experiencing sexuality for the enjoyment of it, or enjoying sex without the intent to procreate new generations of individuals who would become Christian "by water and the Word." However, if an egg was fertilized during intercourse, it was to be acknowledged as a *potential* being—inasmuch as the early church did not accord an unborn fetus a soul and thus recognize its humanity (the Roman Catholic Church did not recognize a fetus as having a soul until the second half of the nineteenth century).

Since two individuals of opposite gender pledged their troth and vowed to remain together for the entirety of their lives, bearing children, and testifying to their religious convictions, the early church prohibited divorce on the grounds that once a pledge was made it could not be unmade.[37] Thus, following the writings of the book allegedly written by the follower Mark, and enshrined in a variety of epigraphia by prophets, disciples, priests, and other men and women acknowledged for or believed to be spiritually inclined, divorce was ruled out regardless of reason or need. When a couple wished to separate it was more commonly the goal of the male rather than of the female, for the female was more oriented towards conforming to the wishes and pronouncements of the *ekklesia*, than were men, and were willing to suffer deprivation and death to adhere to the

[37]Mark 10:1-12.

precepts of law as entoned by the clergy. Because of the adamancy of many wives not to grant their husbands a divorce, the men who felt entrapped in an unhappy or troublesome marriage saw no alternative than to expose their wives' confessions of Christian sentiment and adoption, and bring them to public trial on grounds of being unpatriotic and holding socially dangerous beliefs— which most hagiographers pounced upon as meaning that their crime was that of being a Christian. One Greek record detailing such a situation reads:[38]

> There was a woman married to a man of evil life, in which she too formerly participated; but once she had come to know the teaching of Christ she became reformed and tried to turn her husband by persuasion into reforming his own life: calling to his mind the doctrines of Christ and warning him of the eternal fire prepared for those who do not live according to the discipline and right reason. But the man persisted in his licentiousness and alienated his wife by his actions. His wife then thought that it would be evil to continue to live with a man who sought his pleasures from any source whatsoever, no matter whether it was against justice or natural law. And so she had wished to have her marriage dissolved (*repudium*). Her relatives, however, advised her to remain [with her husband] on the

[38]Justin Martyr, *Apologia* in *Corpus apologetarum christianorum* (Jena, 1879) III:266f. Cf. my *Sex, Woman & Religion* (Dallas, 1984).

ground that her husband might one day attain the hope of amending his ways. So she forced herself to stay with him.

Shortly thereafter her husband left her for [the city of] Alexandria. Word was brought back to her that he was acting worse than he had ever done earlier. Therefore, his wife, not wishing to become an accomplice in his crimes and in his injustices by remaining married to him, sharing his bed and his food, gave him what you call a dissolution [a physical but not legal separation based on proximity] and left him.

Now her excellent husband should have been happy that his wife had given up the practices she formerly used to indulge in so carelessly with servants and hirelings: taking her pleasure in drunkenness and every sort of vice, and that she had even attempted to get him to stop [doing the same]. Instead he filed a complaint against her on the ground that she had left him without his consent, adding that she was a Christian. She then submitted a petition to you, Emperor, asking that she be allowed first to settle her affairs and then, after she had done so, to defend herself against the charge of having left him without his consent. And you granted her petition."

In refusing to grant a husband a total civil divorce, or to refuse a husband "his marriage right"—sex at his desire and time—a woman was seen as being both disobedient to her parents (who were expected to have "taught her the righteous and dutiful paths of young women who are to serve and honor their men above all—even equal to the devotion they show the gods", but also disobedient to the state since their refusal was tantamount to limiting if not ending the man's "right and civic responsibility to bring into this world Romans who can control its destiny." Pagan (or non-Christian) parents were therefore in the forefront of civil litigation against their Christian children, for by allowing their heirs freedom to choose their own philosophical destiny endangered the entire patrimony, the status and reputation of the *gens* and clan, and imperiled the safety of the state—not to mention their own physical well being and longevity.

Women converts, which outnumbered men who converted at first to the Christian message, were especially mourned when their ideological change was made known to their parents. For this reason many parents of Christian women brought their daughters before the tribunals for "justice": which usually was an attempt on the part of the parents to "persuade" their daughters to "return to right reasoning and correct thinking, to honor the gods and the state" and to stay filial in relationship to their progenitors and clan:

"At this my father was so angry with the word 'Christian' that he moved towards me as though he would pluck my eyes out, but be-

...tunc pater motus hoc uerbo mittit se in me ut oculos mihi erueret, sed uexauit tantum et profectus est uictus cum argumentis

---

[39] See my *Passio Sanctarum Perpetuae et Felicitatis: A Translation and Critical Commentary* (Los Angeles, 1975).

fore the Prefect came out against me with devilish arguments."

diaboli.

A similar situation developed among the Christians, with the Christian mothers most adamant over any child of their's desiring to return to the old faith. Instead, Christian mothers encouraged their sons and daughters to "stand fast" and die for the message of Jesus of Nazareth regardless of the pain, the means of death, or the penalties that would be extracted:[40]

"At his side he had a mother of superior character. Her faith gave her a place joined with the patriarchs, showing in this that she was a true daughter of Abraham inasmuch as she wanted her son to be a martyr and was grieved with a sorrow born of pride that his martyrdom was delayed. Ah! mother of such devoted piety! A mother to be numbered among the great saints of old! A mother of the race of

...haerebat lateri eius incomparabilis mater, quae praeter fidem qua ad patriarchas pertineret, in hoc etiam se Abrahae filiam comprobauit, quod filium suum et optabat occidi et quod interim remansisset constristabatur glorioso dolore. O matrem religiose piam! o matrem inter uetera exempla numerandam! o Machabaeicam matrem! nihil enim interest de numero filiorum, cum perinde et haec in

[40]*Passio Sanctorum Montani et Lucii*, from P. Franchi de Cavalieri, "Gli Atti dei SS. Montano, Lucio e compagni," in *Roemische Quartalschrift* 8, Supplementheft (1898) pp. 71-86. Cf. P. Franchi de Cavalieri, "Nuove osservazione critiche ed esegetiche sul testo della Passio Sanctorum Montani et Lucii," in "Note agiografiche, fasc. 3," *ST* 22 (1909) pp. 3-31. Cp. Ruinart, *AM* pp. 275-282, and my *On the* Passio Sanctorum Montani et Lucii: *A Critical Commentary* (Los Angeles, 1976).

the Maccabees! no matter the number of her sons for in like manner she too offered all her love to her Lord in this her only one!

unico pignore totos affectus suos domino mancianimum, ut dilationem suam non doloret. Scis, inquit, mater merito carissima, ut semper temptauerim si confiteri contigiseet, matryrio meo frui et frequenter catentatus uideri et saepe differriri, si ergo contigit quod optuai gloriandum est potius quam dolendum.

Death, in fact, was considered to be a greater comfort to most Christian women than was living. If they could not die, they could experience this "joyous celebration" of death in the martyrdom of their progeny. A near mass-suicidal psychology prevailed, and those who died were praised as champions of a cause, their life's end hailed as "a new beginning," and those who encouraged the martyred to accept their end with "a psalm in their hearts, a song on their lips, and their eyes fixed firmly on the world to come," were saluted salubriously as if they had just returned from a peregrination to the Promised Land filled with milk and honey, cool winds, restful gardens where "both lion and lamb lay down together in harmony." In a world where life's uncertainties abounded, this was more than tempting, and encouraged many Christian mothers to daily preach the joys of "laying down your life for the glory of the Name of Jesus," urging their children "not to be cautious in speech or action when testifying that he [Jesus] has risen" for if they were arrested, tortured, beaten, and put to death, the victims were to "offer it up even as god the Father offered up his only begotten son to suffer and die for us so that we may live forever in his bosom."

One special admonition was given to young girls and to women. Female Christians were told that their most priceless possession cherished by the Christian godhead was their sexual virginity. To preserve this concept of virginity by retaining the hymen was the soul obligation of women who accepted Jesus. Death was therefore preferable to losing the hymen or having even a temporary penial introduction into the vagina, even if the introduction was but cursory, not completed, and marginal. Death, in fact, was believed to be preferred over any sexual intercourse, and a woman who was "endangered by the possibly of losing her sweet viriginity to a man"—be he her groom, a rapist, or any number of men in a brothel, she was instructed to take her life "rather than submit, for the ending of a good life is preferable to being defiled into a bad life." Such action was not considered suicide, but an ultimate demonstration of devotion of love for the Christian godhead, for the avoidance and eschewment of human sexuality was believed to be the only way to untie the ropes of mortality, to file away the strangling chains of the ephemeral, and to end licentiousness, covetousness, and ribald sensuality: a facets of evil forces synthesized and personified in an ogre known as the Devil.

Historically, sex has been condemned in any society by groups of people who feel especially threatened by the society and/or the "forces" within or outside of the society: war, pestilence, religion, innovations and the rejection of tradition and "traditional values." If sex has not been totally condemned and eschewed by the people within the condemning group (such as with the early Christians, or later with Albigensians, and then Shakers in early American history, to name but a few), it is strictly limited and regimented: usually requiring that those who actively participate in sex do so only for "procreation" and then only in ways that the act can lead to regeneration of the human species. Any act that would hinder, limit, or end reproduction has, again historically, been condemned as both an offense against a god and against the state—be the condemnation springing from the misogynistic writings of the Christian apostate Father of the Church Tertullian, Origen (another "Father of the Church" who castrated himself so as not to be drafted into the military), or the contemporary leader of the Radical Religious Right in America: Jerry Falwell, or eighth-grade educated evangelist James Robison.

The women in the early Christian church and community were no different in temperment nor theological ideology than were (and are) these ideologistic demigogues. These terrestial tyrants who spoke as priests and bishops within the church, or lauded nonconventional ideas before quavering and potentially apostacizing progeny argued that sex was an instrument of the Devil who either plunged from heaven following a celestial war the Devil and other evil minions lost, or burst from the base bowels of hell to lead those who engaged in sex—especially promiscuous and rampant sexuality—into the pit of perdition. This pit was far worse than mortals could imagine—or so it was declared.

The adamancy of the foes of human sexuality bothered conventional Romans. Sex was a normal facet of life—and necessary for life, its tensions, and its stability. Christian objections to, and pontifications against sex, appeared to literate Romans as bordering on insanity. Since it was commonly believed that any thought other than that which was commonly expressed was deviant, and deviance from the norm was termed insanity, the Christians were viewed as sociopathic deviants. As sociopathic deviants whose commentary appeared to be testimony of primitive insanity, and since insanity was held to be contagious, the government stepped in to protect the sanity of the nation by erasing the "the root of our troubles, the source of our conflicts—those people who stir up brother against brother, husband against wife, parent against son, and communities against communities." Thus Rome found justification for the genocide of the Christian community.

Sex was used as a punishment against Christians. A virgin woman who was suspected, accused, or proved guilty of the various crimes associated with being a Christian was frequently turned over to a brothel, there to be sexually abused by any client, or gang raped; at other times the woman was farmed out as entertainment and sport to engage in any form of sexuality from beastial to serial with any individual (such as a military hero or military barracks personnel, a religious official, a theatrical, literary, or gladitorial celebrity, and the like) or group which had sufficient gold, political pull, or special status.[41] In many of these cases the virgin woman would commit suicide to "preserve her chastity"—a reality which, although distressing to the Fathers of the Church who argued against the taking of one's life which they felt was an expression of surrendering all hope, they, in instances of this nature, permitted and even lauded as a mark of sainthood—for the woman was "forever retaining her brideshead for the sake of her eternal heavenly groom."[42]

Women who did experience sex, especially even in a sanctified state of matrimony, saw it as a tormenting moment to be pushed into memory with resignation. This was in part because the men of this ancient age had little knowledge on

---

[41]See my *Martyrdom of the Holy Women* as cited.

[42]Eusebius, *MP* 5. Ruinart, *AM*, 143, 395. Cp. Harnack, *CAL* II:475. See also the account of the *Seven Virgins of Ancyra* in Ruinart, *AM: Acta Theodoti*, but approach with caution the martyrdoms of Dionysia (*ibid.*, 160), and Domnina (*ibid.*, 476). Tertullian discusses similar brutalities in his *Apol.*, 50, but note my caveat concerning his commentary in my *Women and Tertullian in the Records of the Early Christian Church* (Toronto: Theological History Press, 1978), pp. 469-512.

the finese and nuances of human sexuality and even less knowledge of the basic mechanics of human sexuality. Thus most women experienced rape by their spouse on the wedding night, and each night that "a man sought his marriage due," the woman "offered it up to the Almighty as one additional cross to bear in order to win eternal life."

With regularity the women in this early age of Christianity who claimed to be confessors of the faith in the Nazarene lamented the act, mourned their personal physical participation, and sometimes during and nearly always afterwards sought penance in fear that they might have enjoyed the act of penial intromission. This overwhelming sense of personal guilt ultimately led numerous women to the convent, other women to suicide, and yet even some women into deliberately seeking martyrdom so that they could be forgiven of an earthly painful pleasure that they were convinced was evil, wrong, and unChristian. Many times these women, in hatred for themselves for having endulged in sex, took not only their own lives but the lives of the unborn, yet to be born, or newly born when they committed suicide, sought martyrdom, were confined to prison, and the like. Those who could not be executed for an alleged crime within the calling of Christianity because they were "with child" lamented the postponement of their fate with a near bitterness, and no regard for the unborn:[43]

---

[43] *Passio Sanctarum Perpetuae et Felicitatis*, as cited, III:8-9, and XV:1-3, with my commentary in *Women and Tertullian in the Records of the Early Christian Church*, Appendix III, p. 789.

...ego infantem lactabam iam inedia defectum; sollicita pro eo adloquebar matrem et confortabam fratrem, commendabam filium; tabescebam ideo quod illos tabescere uideram mei beneficio; tales sollicitudines multis diebus passa sum; et usurpaui ut mecum infans in carcere maneret;et statim conualui et releuata sum a labore et sollicitudine infantis, et factus est mihi carcer subito praetorium, ut ibi mallem esse quam alicubi.

. . . .

Circa Felicitatem...cum octo iam mensium uentrem haberet (nam praegnans fuerat adprehensa), instante spectaculi die in magno erat luctu ne propter uentrem differretur (quia non licet praegnantes poenae repraesentari) et ne inter alios postea sceleratos sanctum et innocentem sanguinem funderet, set et con martyres grauiter constristabantur ne tam bonam sociam quasi comitem solam in uia eiusdem spei relinquerent.

I [Perpetua] nursed my baby who was faint from hunger. In my anxiety I spoke to my mother about the child. I tried to comfort my brother, and I gave the child to their keeping. I was in pain because I saw them suffering out of pity for me. These were the trials I had to endure for my days. Then I got permission for my baby to stay with me in prison. At once I recovered my health, relieved as I was out of worry and anxiety for my child. My prison had suddenly become a palace, so that I wanted to be there rather than anywhere else.

. . . .

As for Felicitas...she had been pregnant when she was arrested, and she was now in her eighth month. As the day of the spectacle drew near she was very distressed that her martyrdom would be postponed because she was pregnant: for it is against the law for women with child to be executed. Thus she might have to shed her holy, innocent blood afterwards with others who were common criminals....

Numerous Christian women were exposed pregnant to the elements, wild animals, gladiators, and other a host of other predators. The impact of their physical exposure however was marginal both in concern with the general viewing populace who found it more entertaining than distressing, and among the Christians who, for the most part, in spite of what martyrologists claim in the zeal of their religious testimonies, found it to be an extreme expression—with many fleeing to the hills and distant lands to avoid martyrdom.[44] Most Christian women, rather than encouraging their children to seek out the "glory of martyrdom," or offering them up to the Roman hosts to become martyrs, instead urged their children to hide.[45]

The exception, as in all climes and times, was more tantilizing as fodder for gossip and for fueling speculation and genophobia. Thus the occasional woman who would either demand to be executed in testimony of her faith, or offered up her children as "examples for those of the faith to be firm and hold fast," made the general populace and the Roman government question the sanity of the new minor cult that came in from the Middle East. Rumors abounded as to what the Christian women really were. Since many began to dress like men, crop their hair (which was seen as a sign of prostitution in Jerusalem and similarly perceived in other communities, leading Saul of Tarsus [St. Paul] to write out against women coming into community gatherings with their hair un-

---

[44]See my *Woman in the Age of Christian Martyrs*, as cited, p. 27.

covered—not because there was anything wrong with the woman's position in the community group, but because it was adding scandal to an already volatile situation and thus adding fuel to the fires of anti-Christian sentiment), and speak out in an "unladylike manner," Roman detractors declared that the Christians were at best allamorphic or androgynous, and possibly transvestites to transsexual eunuchs. At the same time the Christians were accused of being orgists, intemperate, non-social, and ahedonistic.[46] These highly irregular and unorthodox moves made many worry about their safety and that of their family members, especially the children.

---

[46]Eusbius, *MP* 11, and his *HE* VIII:9. Cf. Genhardt, *AMS* 64-6.

The Martyrdom of St. Catherine of Alexandria
(Giovanni Da Milano)

Charges Against the Christians

The most common charge against the early Christians was that of atheism. Since Christians did not recognize the established state gods, Rome held that the Christians did not accept the gods, and thus were atheists ("without god").

Christian women, moreso than Christian men, delighted in the charge of being atheists. Much of their enthusiasm came because of the preaching of firebrands who demanded a rejection of the establishment and its deities in order to show their own devotion to Jesus. Tertullian, for example, claimed that to accept the traditional gods of Rome would be tantamount to worshipping the imps of Satan and thereby forfeit the immortal soul. At the same time this one-time Father of the Church who later abjured Roman Christianity, detailed how women would win the "crown of immortality" by defying the common law of Rome which demanded that they sacrifice to the *gens* of the emperor or be guilty of both treason and sacrilege: *crimen laesae Romanae religionis.* The penalty for the crime of treason and sacrilege was death by execution.[47]

Not only did Christians in general reject the gods of Rome, but Christian women especially rallied against the gods, overtly attacked the deities statues and temples, publicly preached against them in the streets and the market place, and desecrated their altars along the road side. Furthermoreso than men, early Christian women attacked and ridiculed the followers of "the old

---

[47]Tert., *Apol.* 24.

gods," laughed at the testimony of faith by those who accepted the traditional deities, and were publicly insolent to the clergy of the state religion, making themselves not only increasingly unpopular even with the poor and uneducated, but appearing as a threat against the established order, law and Roman justice.

Early Christian women intensified their attacks on the old gods the closer they believed they were coming to their own trials and execution. Not only did they denounce the gods of Rome, but preached with the power of Paul about the existence of what they believed to be a single god—an advocacy which was beyond the common comprehension (*deus unicus, solitarius, destitutus...*)[48] Not only did these early Christian women attack the plurality of the pantheon of gods, but the faith of those who still defended them, declaiming the followers of the deities and worshippers of the *gens* of the emperor "low life" and "illiterate"—claims which were not understood[49] nor appreciated by the general populace who saw the early Christians as "poor rabble and slaves" the majority of who had no formal learning and many who could barely operate in an intelligible manner. Thus the Christian attack upon the followers of the gods of Rome as being "illiterate" and "low born ... of low life" appeared ludicrous at best.

---

[48]Tert., *ibid.*, 22ff, and his *de Spectac* 13. Origen, *Cels.* III:35, VII:69 *et passim.* Ruinart, *AM*, 545-548. For the Roman view on the Christian attack on state temples, see Caecilius in *Minuc. Felix* **Oct.** 8. See also my *Woman of Ancient Rome* (1980), and my *Rome's Attitude Towards the Early Christian Community* (Toronto: Theological History, 1979).

[49]Porphyry in Marcarius Magnes, *Apocritica* IV:29. Harnack, *EC* I:291n. My *Gods of Ancient Rome and the Christian Faith* (Denison: Apologia Christianorum, 1977).

The sharpness with which the Christian apologists denounced the gods and the numerous unfounded charges they leveled against the Old Believers while refusing to explain their own strange customs and ways or define the fundamentals (not to mention the base adiaphora) of their faith added fuel to the growing fire of intolerance that burned in the hearts of the Roman intelligencia, eruditii, and common person.[50] Questions were asked of the Christians—and the Christians refused to respond with any civility, only offering a bitterly biting testimony of their own faith which for the most part went unexplained. Answers, the early Christians argued, could only be obtained if the questioner truly desired to adopt the faith, would willingly undergo a rigid period of training in the faith, and affirm an unqualified willingess to witness to the faith if necessary by sacrificing his or her life to "the enemies of Christ" which meant primarily to eschew Rome and its laws and thus to abandon the basic Roman society in favor of an underground or clandestine community. Few Romans, proporitionate to the population, agreed to such unbending demands and so stayed clear of becoming catechumens.

One of the most dramatic reasons why many Romans avoided Christians, and refused to matriculate in the catechatical courses offered by various ministers and deacons—many of whom were women—was because of the popular misconception of the Christian community's participation in the Eucharist. Since the Christians

---

[50]Eusebius, *HE* V:1.3-2.8.

came from celebrating the Eucharist declared with joy that they had "eaten the body and drank the blood" of their god, the general concensus was that the Christians were cannibals.[51] Not only was the idea of cannibalism repulsive to the Romans, but numerous citizens feared that the Christians were dining strictly and solely on the flesh of young children and infants inasmuch as the women who carried infants and small toddlers into the houses of compatriots for worship, praise, and baptism, frequently left to get additional bread and wine, singing the words, "Except you eat my flesh and drink my blood, you have no life in yourself"—a hymn with emphasis quite similar to psalms of praise found in the fastly growing cults of Mithra and Cybele where a bull was sacrificed, the worshippers bathed in and drank its blood, and at times consumed its flesh.[52]

When the women returned bearing bread and wine, declaring that they were entering into a love feast, further questions surfaced, but little was said for the common quandry was the fate of the children who were to be involved in the same experience. When the infants and children were not brought out with the women when the women left the love feast, the charge of cannibalism quickly became vocal—a charge few Christian women deemed worthy of an answer, and thus walked by their accusers in silence with a "glow on their face, a smile on their lips, and a radiance in their every move." Even though the infants and

---

[51]*Ibid.*

[52]Tert. *de Praescript.* 40. Macarius Magnes, *Apocritica* III:15.

children had been left behind to be trained in the faith, to receive baptism, or to be instructed in the teaching ministry by the elderly and were returned home late in the night by silent figures who hugged dark walls mutely proceeding as if they were without common cognizance, the charge of cannibalism of the children by the women was frequently launched against a woman or several women collectively. If the woman refused to answer the charge or if she failed to produce the suspected victim to the court she would be given the death penalty not only for alleged murder but also cannibalism, which caused the woman to whisper to a co-religionist to keep and maintain the child or to spirit the child out of the city in which she was to die.[53]

After the death of the woman, the child was frequently hailed as the product of a living martyr and encouraged "to like commitment" at the next love feast. The Romans labeled this love fete as a "Thyestean feast" which was considered a spawning ground for either Oedipodean intercourse or homosexual orgy. Since women and their children made up the strength of the individual congregations, and they returned to their homes acclaiming "what a great love we have shared" the assumption of an Oedipodean relationship between the women and their children is understandable. So too must we understand the Romans' belief that the early *agapes* of the Christians was a homosexual orgy inasmuch as the sexes separated upon entering the congregational confines, exchanged there (and in public)

[53]*DCB* III:767.

the *osculum pacis* (kiss of peace) as was instituted by St. Paul, delighted in revering the separation of the sexes and yet acclaiming that "there is neither male nor female" so that gender recognition and acceptance seemed outside of the Christian community's comprehension, causing the Romans to see the ritual as preceeding an orgy of great proportions: *quos per flagitia ivisos vulgus Chrestianaos* [sic] *appallabat.*[54]

Other Roman concerns of the early Christians' attitude towards human sexuality flourished after the first generation when the separation between the men and women was erased. With the erasure came speculation that constant sexual orgies were being held. This thesis was supported by the event which most Romans were aware of: that first the women, and then the men, met at night in a secret manner in a dark place there to "perform the act of love" (penance). Since such secret activities were against the Roman law, the continued participation of the early Christians in this "act of love" was ruled as treason (*collegium illicitum*) and was punishable by death.

These illicit meetings were even more feared after the burning of Rome by Nero. The cry quickly arose that not only were the Christians responsible for the conflagration, but that the gods of Rome allowed the holocaust to spread since the innovations of the Christians was a direct insult to their sacred divinity and a thinly veiled threat of conspiracy against the state. The Christian god offended the true gods, and the fire was their

---

[54]Suetonius, *Caes.* 42, Oct. 32. Dio Cass. LIII:36; cf. Ulpian, *Digest* XLII:22, 2 and XLVIII:4,1. Cp. Paulus, *Sent.* V:29. Tacticus, *Annales* XV:44.

response to such mockery and heresy, brought on and encouraged by Christian women who were, it appeared to many, stirring up rebellion in the homes of good Romans: *quasi molitoris rerum novarum.*[55] Christians had to go!

Innovations were especially feared by the Romans, especially as the empire increasingly became a more heterogenous habitat for a nonhomogenous people. The unique entity of being "a Roman" gave way to being a part of an expanding empire, and later merged into a special group consciousness among the followers of the teachings of the Nazarene who saw themselves as a part of *corpus Christianorum* which was believed to be even greater than the Eternal Empire of Imperial Rome, a philosophy and identity which terrified the traditional heritage-minded Roman who refused to acknowledge any thing to be greater than Rome. The wanton and senseless destruction of Roman temples and statues of Roman deities by the Christians who lauded such barbaric and intolerant behavior while scorning and ridiculing religious processions in honor of the empire's growing number of gods or celebrating martial victories by the state over Rome's enemies made the Christians even more despised. Such inhospitable and uncharitable behavior as the Christians expressed brought about additional and increasing demands for their removal from society—by persecution and liquidation if necessary.[56]

Roman persecutions of the Christians did not

---

[55]Livy, XXXIX:8f. Eusebius, *op. cit.* III:18. *CIL* VI:948. Suet. *Dom.* 10, 15, 17.

[56]*PG* III:735-748. Cf. *PL* LXXIV:211.

lessen nor dull their ardor. Instead as the persecutions escalated, Christians—especially women—intensified their hostilities towards the empire and towards non-Christians, openly challenging the *status quo*—action which firmed the hatred of Christians by the majority of Rome's citizens.

The bitterness and anger felt towards Christians by non-Christian Rome reached a volatile point when Christian women rejected the traditional concept of *familia* by refusing to marry their father's choice if the man was not a Christian. As Christians, the women believed that if they were to marry it was their Christian duty to marry a Christian man.[57] Such independence, such a demand for freedom of choice, was unheard of and was not going to be tolerated.

If Christian women did marry non-Christian men the marriage not only proved to be disruptive of the lives of the two individuals involved, but the Christian woman was seen as an exceedingly overbearing and overwhelmingly bad neighbor. Seldom did she develop a community or neighborhood consciousness. Instead she took every free opportunity to proselytize her faith, entering into her neighbor's domestic quarrels and urging if not both parties, at least one or the other to abjure their faith, abandon the marriage, and follow the teachings of Jesus Christ. For this form of interference the Greeks had a special word: Ἀλλοτριοεπίσκοπος.[58]

Christian women in the early church did not

---

[57]Harnack, *EC* II:235-238.

[58]Ramsay, *ChE* 293n. Le Blant, *ICG* I:126, based on Matt. 23:9. Ruinart, *op. cit.* 385.

respect traditional lines of family ties and authority if the family they were with, either their own or
another individual's, was not a member of the
Christian community. Christians in Gaul refused
to call any man "father"—reserving that title for
the Christian diety and that deity's priesthood. At
the same time the standard and accepted heirar-
chy of the temporal family was ignored or rudely
brushed aside, forcing many non-Christians in
Gaul to charge their relatives, family, and friends
with incivility, going against tradition, and being a
threat to society "as these Christians neither
recognize nor do they respect" customary rank
and authority, their place in the family or community, the cry went out.[59]

If a spouse became an "apostate"—or, fell
back into the non-Christian faith of his or her
youth—the Christian spouse frequently left the
house, although that spouse did not always sue
for a divorce. Divorce, however, was not out of the
question. Christian leaders were not always hesi-
tant to sever the union which "man has put
together—defining that to mean "by the hands of
pagan priests blaspheming the true god Jesus
Christ"—whereas they were slow in dissolving
any bond of matrimony they had officiated over,
or was conducted between two consenting Christians.

Not only did the Christian spouse feel compell-
ed to leave an apostacized Christian, but when
the separation occured, the Christian spouse frequently claimed and took possession of most of
the family goods. Once the property had been se-

[59]Tert. *ad Scap.* 3.

questered, much of it was disposed of by dividing it among co-believers or distributing it among the poor during a missionary crusade for new members.

Christian women were not desirable neighbors. This was especially true when they were married to non-Christian men, for they refused, for the most part, to recognize and respect the *patria potestas* of the father in determining the course, evolution and propagation of the family: whether or not she had a child, and once, if the child was conceived, carried and was born into this world, whether or not the child lived.

Universally Christian women opposed both abortion and infanticide—practices increasingly less common in the ancient Roman world, but not one that was totally estranged from reality. Because of this, those women who did not encourage their children to seek martyrdom, or beg to be martyred while the fetus was still developing within their womb, frequently offered their children to the executioner with the plea that it be taken care of and loved. Generations earlier, before Christian women came to Rome or began to multiply in the empire—even before the advent of Jesus of Nazareth—Roman husbands had total control over the wife's body and her reproductive prowess. If he wanted a child she had nothing to say. If he wanted to dispose of a fetus or a child, she was required by custom and law to do away with the unwanted.

The emergence of self-expression among Christian women intensified even beyond her insistence on maintaining and sustaining her body and the free-will upkeep of it. This self-assertion carried over into areas beyond the family circle and governance. It ripened in the social world of festivals which neophytes and women priests of the early Roman Catholic church labored at turning into Christian holidays complete with adiaphoric drenched worship services inaugerating the veneration of some spectacular martyr living or dead who was publicly acclaimed a holy person—or saint.[60]

With the public recognition of a martyr's deed of witnessing to the faith of Jesus as expressed in word or act came the call by early Christian women that death and dying and subsequent burial be turned into a solemn religious service of mourning and remembrance. Women dominated in all areas, from attending the vigil of a co-religionist's final passing, to sealing the deceased eyes' with a sign of the cross and the sprinkling of holy water, to the preparation for burial. Furthermore, it was the women who determined where the dead would be buried. If a husband and wife died at the same time, and both were recognized as communicant Christians, deaconesses from the church demanded that the two be buried together. If only one of the two who died was a Christian, these same deaconesses rigidly ruled that only the Christian could be buried in Christian-sanctified ground regardless of the wishes of the family of the deceased. Such insensitivity in the name of religion frequently brought with it the renunciation of Christianity by the offended family members or the estrangement of the family who divided over the issue on fundamental religious grounds.

[60]Tert. *ad Uxor.* II:4,5. Arnobius, *Adv. Gent.* II:5.

The exclusive exclusion of non-Christians from select burial grounds sanctified by Christians led to the separation of many families. Husbands left wives more frequently than did wives leave husbands inasmuch as the majority of the earliest converts were women who found great comfort in the message of a better life after death than could be found in the traditional Roman home and society. On the other hand Roman men found glory in the war maneuverings of the empire which they either directly participated in or were made to feel a part with the splendid triumphal parades, rich rhetoric justifying the barbaric and needless slaughter of innocent lives for the sake of expansion and the glorification of an already too enlarged imperial ego. Crazed for war and determined to pilot the politics and philosophies of conquered people, Rome demanded that those living outside of the City follow its dictates. There was little concern about the human body, and far less about the soul which was considered at best an illusive illumination, and at worse a non-entity. To quarrel over either body or soul seemed absurd. It was also socially dissettling. Thus when a Christian wife admonished her husband to prepare for the "next existence" most men saw her ministrations as audacious and even as insane. If her pleas and demands became increasingly annoying and sharply acute, the wife could be taken before a civil magistrate to divorce her, have her committed to an asylum, or to have her put to death on the charge of disrupting the settlement of the empire. If the husband tolerated the boisterous wife and lived to die in the matrimonial bonds with the Christian, the Christian wife would spend time not mourning the passing of the mate as was traditional in Roman society, but instead spend numerous hours preparing the cadaver for burial. In doing so, the Christian wife greatly distressed her husband's parents, threatening his patrimony. Numerous records exist detailing how the distraught family of the deceased, after praying the widow to cease her calloused preparations which they did not understand nor appreciate, carried her to court to complain to the authorities that she was showing no respect to their lossed loved one, nor to the state and sacred traditions, all of which could lead to her being cursed as a Christian and rabble rouser deserving of death.[61]

The unique aspect of the death and burial was not the only dissettling phenomena that injured social consciousness, for the widow would in most cases in the early days of the emerging church take all that the husband had left to her and distribute it equally among the faithful of her congregation and to the poor of the streets.[62] This rank communism not only offended the materialistic philosophy of the time but enraged the husband's family who saw his work being thwarted and his goods taken from the patrimony. Cries of outrage were common—and effective, for within a generation after the death of the landless and impoverished itinerant lecturer from Galilee, the man born at Nazareth, his followers began to retain and augment and increase their earthly possessions until they were among the growing number of new rich. A few of these "other-world"

---

[61]Le Blant, *loc. cit.*

[62]Acts 2:44-47, 4:34-35.

oriented Christians in fact owned other human beings; what separated them from the traditional slave owners of Rome was that early Christian slave owners were more just in their treatment of their human property in the areas of labor, protection, sustaining and clothing the body—but, at the same time less tolerant of what their slaves believed, for it was customary to force the conversion of the entire slave population once the owner decided to adopt the Christian credo and accept the Christian faith. Slaves which were not agreeable to taking on the teaching of the Nazarene were frequently sold. Those slaves, however, which accepted Christianity were treated quite well, and if they showed a propensity and interest in the furthering of the message of Jesus, they could be, with the blessings of their owner, ordained a deacon/ess, priest/ess, or even bishop: a unique social revolution that was not frequently practiced in the ancient world by many faiths.[63] This "leveling" process—the acceptance of a slave on equal footing with a free person, was most distressing to class conscious Romans.

Christian women were generally the most zealous in destroying class distinctions, believing firmly in the words of St. Paul "that there is neither free nor slave, neither male nor female, neither Jew nor Gentile...." To this end many wealthy Christian women not only freed their own slaves but even went into the market place to buy those who were already enslaved in order to

[63]Duchesne, LP I:132 n.4; and my Woman in the Apostolic Age (33-107 A.D.) (Mesquite: Ide House, 1980); my The Teachings of Jesus on Women (Dallas: Texas Independent Press, 1984); and my On the Ordination of Women (Las Colinas: The Liberal Press, 1985).

emancipate them as well. This was especially goading to the Roman aristocracy who not only feared a classless society which would spell the downfall of major patrician households, but more so increase the possibility of a class warfare where the slaves who were still under the yoke of a private owner would rise up in the manner of Spartacus in revolt for their own freedom.

The classical classless communism as practiced by the early Christians became even more objectionable when several leading spokespersons for the early movement began advocating practioneers of the faith to eschew all forms of property and trappings of wealth in order to be free to take a vow of life-long poverty and self-denial. This appeared to the non-Christian Roman as a degradation of the traditional Roman attitude towards the superiority of the free over the unfree, and placed many a native born Roman citizen on the same low level as a slave. Such an assumption was confirmed, in the minds of many Roman citizens, when the Roman Christians took the vow of abstinence and poverty, sharing the slave's ancieties, deprivations, and scorn—eating their meager and bland food, wearing their simple rustic clothing, drinking only water or cheap wine, and working side by side in an atmosphere of confraternity.[64]

Christians who labored beside slaves on an equal footing with the slaves brought a salvo of outcry from the parched and embittered throats of the Roman business community. They told civil

[64]Hippolytus, *Philos.* IX:12. Cf. Wallon, *Histoire d'Esclavage dans l'Antiquite (Paris, 1879 2d ed., 3 vols.).* Cp. *I Cor.* 7:21.

judges and magistrates that the Christians were actually working against the gods, since the gods of the heavens showed their favor upon the just of the earth by rewarding them with largesses and increasing testimonials of wealth indicative of their election to the rank of being "near the gods, fashioned like the gods"—a thesis on election being reflected in personal prosperity that was foreign to the early Christians. They recalled Christ's statement that "it is more difficult for a rich man to enter into heaven than it is for a camel to go through the eye of a needle," and, also, "lay not up treasures on earth for your soul may be required in heaven"—a thesis that was confirmed as the message of Christ until the Protestant Revolution when the one-time French priest Jean Calvin returned to the thinking of the Roman patricians and declared that a demonstration of God's love for a "righteous soul" could be measured in the blessings that the individual realized on earth—that work leading to wealth showed one's election to the chosen number who would occupy heaven.

The argument over ownership of property and other testimonies of wealth alienated factions within the society and people within factions. This alienation of society produced a spawning of articulate and indiscreet fanatics who showed utter contempt for their fellow humans in their preachifications and declamations, lacking basic charity not only in their words but in their deportment and deeds.[65] Their bristling bitterness quick-

† = *Origen, Cels.* VII:9, 11.

[66]Vergil, *Georg* II:490-492. Tert. *Apol.* 47. Hermas, *Shep. Vis.* IV:3.

ly attracted pseudo-religious imposters: men and women who adopted the colors of Christianity to fly banners that were void of basic Christian ideals but sounded good enough to win some converts while enriching the charlatans. Many well meaning Christians urged co-religionists to tolerate these infidels on the assumption that a greater display of Christian love and forgiveness for their errors would turn these protomachiavellians around and make them into true Christians. The opposite happened. Rome became increasingly intolerant and looked at all Christians and pseudo-Christians in the same way and with the same perspective: declaring the entire group to be outlaws and therefore outside of the protection of the law.[66] From this point in time it was but a short step to declaring the Christian community anarchists. Christianity spearheaded disruptive forces within the empire in much the same base manner as the Zealots engaged in clandestine revolution in Israel with the avoid purpose of overthrowing the empire regardless of cost in time, men, material, and suffering.

Quick action was taken by the empire against this disruptive element. And the action was severe, for Rome would not tolerate covert rebellion within its house.[67]

Christians were noticeably "peculiar". Their dress was different, their hairstyles cut short like a slave, their speech droll and rustic, and their attitudes proudly paraded against the common concensus. Since they were by choice an exclusive

---

[67]Gregory of Nyssa, *Oratio de Theodoro Martyre* in *PG* III:735-748. Cf. *PL* LXXIV:221.

and separate people, they were also seen as seditious in addition to being considered anarchists—one more reason why the empire came down hard on the members of their society. This exclusiveness became more prominent when the leaders of the community, especially the articulate women priests of the ancient church, forbade the congregants to wear distinctive jewelry or any display of jewerly or other trappings of wealth. With the support of the deaconesses and female priests, the most gifted literary minds of the ancient church penned numerous admonitions against conspicuous display and enjoyment of wealth and "fine items."[68] These writings made a major impact on non-ordained and ordained women who sold their jewels to feed the poor, who took to wearing homespun so as not to offend the poor, and who walked so that the lame might ride.

So as not to be conspicuous, Christian women began to stay inside of their dwellings for longer periods of time, seldom venturing out in the day light hours, usually going about their errands at night time. Rather than lower suspicion, this action aroused concern for it gave credence to the belief that the women were plotting new arson attacks upon the city, or inciting riots against the patricians as well as numerous other treasonous acts.[69]

Since the early Christian women were especially impolitic in the choice and use of their words, the fears of the Romans were dramatically

---

[68]Clem. Alex. *Paed.* II:10-III:3, 11.

[69]Minucius Felix, *Oct.* 8.

escalated, especially when they heard the women refer to themselves as "the newly caught," denying all standard codes of conduct and behavior. Furthermoreso, the terms Christian women applied to themselves were identical to the names assumed by terrorist movements within the empire, with many of the firebrands declaring that they were "newly caught" up in a whirlwind of rebellion for the sake of independence.[70]

As the charges were leveled against the Christian community with escalating regularity, the women of the community took less interest in their daily affairs. Referring to themselves as "temporary sojourners," and "sojourners in time" without explaining the reason for their passive listlessness and indifference,[71] while babbling incoherently ("speaking in tongues") using disjointed sections of Christian scripture without fleshing out any theological argument, apology or exegesis—but such was not yet the character of the Christian community for academics remained in the domain of the non-Christian philosophers and writers.[72]

Tertullian explained the common civil opinion of this situation, concurring by declaring that Christians were of little use in public affairs (*infructuosi in negotiia*).[73] In truth, the Christians

---

[70]Tert. *Bapt.* 1.

[71]*Ep. Diognetus* c.5

[72]Psuedo-Cyprian, *de Specta*, 1-2. Tert. *de Idol.* 14. Tertullian admits that this behavior set Christians apart to their detriment: *licet extranei a turbis aestimemur*, in his *Apol.* 31.

[73]Tert. *ibid., Apol.* 42.

were "turning the world upside down."[74]

Because of their sheer obstinancy in refusing to consider anything that was not in line with their rigid orthodoxy (κατὰ ψιλὴν παράταξιν, ὡς οἱ χριστιανοί)[75] Rome felt it necessary to "erase the menace to peace, the home, the family, all to save the children"—cries demigogues have sounded for centuries against that element in their individual societies they did not understand, appreciate, or tolerate due to mutual ignornance and the lack of desire to discover the fullness of each others magnificence expressed in its individual and collective diversity. To spare the lives of the Christians, it was popularly argued, would cost the empire more than it could bear. Depravity would increase as the Christians continued to speak out against tradition and established practices in the home, the market place, the government and the military. Such depravity was simply treason and Rome was unwilling to entertain the continued and rising expense and luxury of condoning it much longer.

Outside of occasional and randomly sporadic persecutions, the empire officially followed a line of tolerance with the Christians. This program of tolerance inspired many moderate Romans to accept the Christian faith. Their numbers increased as the membership in the church escalated with many converts coming from the military, govern-

---

[74]Acts 17:6.

[75]Marcus Aurelius, *Medit.* XI:3.

[76]Origen, *Cels.* IV:23. Pliny, *Ep.* X:96 refers to them as *superstitio prava et immodica.* Cp. Minuc. Felix, *op. cit.* 10.

ment, arts, and legal profession. Christianity became a fad. Joining the church was fashionable and many accepted baptism in order to meet the newest craze and be associated with those who were looked upon as "unique".[77]

By the third century the imperial attitude changed. Tolerance was no longer a hallmark of administration since the empire was being beset on all fronts by disenchanted and dissettled people.

The official attitude was that the Christians were a 'fifth column' of subversives whose goal was to destroy the empire and traditional values. Christians referred to themselves as "the third race"—a title which indicated separativeness and separation within an empire which prided itself on being a unified whole and an unifying force for world peace: *pax Romana*. To go against this official concensus was treason.[78]

The emperors had to act against the Christians by popular demand. To say that the persecutions were solely the result of imperial tyranny is as wrong as to say that all those who died in the persecutions were martyred for their belief in Jesus of Nazareth. The cry "How long must we endure this third race (*usuque quo genus tertium*)," rose daily from the crowds who assembled before the Senate.[79] The government, as representatives and protectors of the people, had to act. Law, tradition, and common sentiment forced the

[77]Eusebius, *HE* I:4.

[79]*Ibid.*

government's hand—the treasury was nearly exhausted, and many Christians were exceedingly wealthy, so that if they were brought to trial for a crime which could lead to their death then their properties and other forms of riches could legally be confiscated by the government and its largesses put into the state treasury to help bail out the empire from near bankruptcy.[80]

[80]Christian women were especially wealthy which helps to account for the number of women who were martyred. See Tert. *du culte feminarium* II:13, and Clem. Alex. *Paed.* II:12, with commentary in my *Tertullian and Woman in Early Christianity* as cited.

The Virgin of Sorrows
(Juan De Juni)

The Persecutions

Greed, fear, desperation and necessity all were determining factors in the imperial Roman persecution of "that hated sect of petty-minded people known as Christian." Although the majority of the executions took place from the third to the fifth centuries CE, the first woman to suffer and die who is recognized as a Christian witness (or martyr) was Pomponia Graecina. She was ostracized from her home in 64 CE, during the reign of Nero (born 37 CE, reigned 54-68 CE).[81]

Pomponia was arraigned before the Roman senate in 57 CE on the charge of holding "a subversive and dangerous foreign superstition" that "brought confusion and concern to many. She was undoubtedly an articulate spokesperson of her cult, and may have been one of its priests. But her claim to fame and remembrance in the Roman church is owing to her acceptance of death at the hands of non-Christian Rome.[82]

Pomponia was not a martyr in the generally understood sense of the word *murtus* (a Greek word for "witness") since she did not surrender her life for her beliefs. She countered her accusers, testified to her faith by an unique act of total silence—and was spared. Pomponia said nothing to her tormentors about the alleged orgies and cannibalistic feasts she was supposed to have indulged in. She returned an icy stare when interrogated concerning her sheltering co-

---

[81]C. Wandinger, *Pomponia Graecina* (Muenchen, 1873) 30ff.

[82]Cf. I Pet. 4:14-16; II Tim. 2:8; Acts 28:21-22. Cf. Lightfoot, *Clem.* I:30-2.

religionists.

Following Pomponia's acquital—due to lack of evidence and the testimony of credible witnesses, Pomponia adopted a life style of perpetual mourning: *longa huic Pomponiae aetas et continua tristitia fuit . . . per quadraginta annos non cultu nisi lugubri non animo nisi maesto egit.*[83]

Few women were as lucky as Pomponia. If they escaped the vengeance of the courts, few were able to survive the vendetta of the people who milled around awaiting the verdict.

The majority of Christian women who were sentenced to die were executed for their constant refusal to make sacrifice to the state and to the emperor's *gens*. The state did not require them to offer religious sacrifice or to invoke any particular diety; the requirement was "to make sacrifice for the peace and prosperity of Mother Rome and for her children...." Refusal to sacrifice for peace was seen as treason: *Supplica, miserere infanti!*[84] and, *fac sacrum pro salute imperatorum.*[85]

It was commonly believed that Christians who refused to sacrifice to the *gens* of the emperor were not only offending the state but also the gods whose help the poor and downtrodden prayed to; by not sacrificing to the gods, the

---

[83]Tacticus, *Annals* XIII:32.

[84]*Passio Sanctarum Perpetuae et Felicitatis* VI:2 with commentary in my translation and discussion appearing in *On the Passions of Virgin Women* as cited.

[85]*Ibid.* 3. Donata agreed to honor Caesar but refused to pray to Caesar: *Honorem Caesari quasi Caesari; timorem autem Deo, in Passio Sanctorum Scillitanorum* 9 as contained in Ruinart, *op. cit.* 131-132. See also the dialogue between Rusticus and Justin, in P. Fanchi de' Cavalieri, "Note agiografiche, 6°" *ST* 33 (1920) 5-17.

thought continued, natural calamities would hit the land with fury: the sky would withhold its rain, there would be earthquakes, fires, famine, pestilences, "and every form of evil."[86] When no rain fell on North Africa for an unseasonably long period of time it was blamed on the state's tolerance of the Christians.[87] Not only did the Roman citizens of North Africa petition the senate in Rome to take immediate action to correct "this offense against the true gods" but they were also joined by numerous other citizens throughout the empire who cried out that if the state did not "rid this land of these people, the accursed Christians," then the entire state would "experience the displeasure of the true gods as do our brothers" in North Africa, lamenting that when this occured the entire empire would crumple.[88]

This "will of the people" to spare the state of a series of calamities was the official argument Nero used when he charged the Christians with the arson of Rome.[88] Those who did survive his persecutions, which were among the most mild in form and number, had a modicum of peace under Flavian, but those believers which persevered to the time of Domitian were greeted with psychopathic barbarities. Convinced that the tolerance of Christianity was the cause for the continuing and increasing troubles of Rome, Domitian, in a grand style, tortured "the enemies

---

[86]Tert. *Apol.* 40, and his *ad Nat.* 9.

[87]Augustine, *Civ. Dei* II:3. Cp. Cyprian, *ad Demetr.* 2; Eusebius, *HE* IV:13, with Nero's charge in 26, and an enlargement by Maximin in IX:7. Cf. *Clementine Hom.* VII:9.

[88] Pliny, *Eps.* 96-97.

of the state" with a finese equaled only by the Marquis de Sade.

To prepare his victims for their "final glory" he set up death banquets:[89]

> At this time he feasted the populace as described; and on another occasion he entertained the foremost men among the senators and military leaders in the following fashion: he prepared a room that was pitch black on every side: ceiling, walls and floors, and had made ready bare couches of the same color which were set on the bare floor. Then he invited his guests alone at night without their attendants. First he sat beside each of them a slab shaped like a gravestone: bearing the guest's name, and also with it a small lamp such as hang in tombs. Next came naked boys who were also painted black. They entered the room like ghosts and after circling the guests in a breath-taking dance took up their stations at their feet. After this all the items that are commonly offered at the sacrifices to the dead spirits were set well before the guests: each of the items being black and set in black dishes. Consequently, every single guest feared and trembled and was kept in constant expectation of having his throat cut at any moment, the more so on the part of everybody else, too—but Domitian; there was dead silence as if they were already in the realms of the dead. The emperor himself conversed only upon topics relating to death and slaughter. Finally he dismissed them—but only after he had sent away

[89] Dio Cass., *op. cit.* LXVII:9-10., the entire Greek text is in my *Woman in the Age of Christian Martyrs*, pp. 42-44.

their slaves who had stood in the
vestibule—and gave his guests to the
custody of other slaves whom they did
not know, to be conveyed either in car-
riages or litters, and by this procedure
he filled them with far greater fear. Then
sacrcely had each guest reached his
own home and was beginning to
breathe easier, as one might say, when
word was brought to him that a
messenger from the Augustus had arriv-
ed. While each one of the guests ac-
cordingly expected to perish this time
in any case, one person brought in the
slab which of silver, and then others in
turn brought in various articles including the dishes that had been set before
them at the dinner: each which was con-
structed of costly material; and then
last of all [came] that particular boy who
had been each guest's familiar ghost,
now washed and adorned. Thus after
having passed the entire night in terror
they received the gifts.

Such was the triumphal celebration,
or, as the crowd put it, such was the
funeral banquet that Domitian held for
those who had died in Dacia and Rome.
Even at this time, too, he slew some of
the foremost men. And in the case of a
certain man who buried the body of one
of the victims, he deprived him of his
property because it was on his estate
that the victim had died.

Domitian was among the most colorful sadistic
persecutors in history. What happened to his ad-
visors and friends, the foremost men of his day,
made the Christians tremble at the thought of
what lay before them when Domitian turned his

anger against "that accursed sect." The persecutions of Domitian, however, were not as systematic and encompassing as those of Trajan whose resolve was more conclusive and his vengeance more swift and sure. Trajan slew an innumerable host of Christians—not because of their faith in the message of the Nazarene—but on the grounds that the Christians were "dividing the empire," encouraging "the [Roman non-Christian] faithful to abandon the worship of the gods, neglect the temples, and insult the priests of the divine faith"; and, refusing to trade in sacrificial animals which was a significant source of revenue for the temple and for the empire.

Once more women were the prime target. Pliny details the importance of persecuting women, given in his detailed examination of two slave women (*ancillae*) who were deaconesses in the early church, preparing for the Christian priesthood.[90] Pliny's only conclusion was that the women suffered under "degrading and irrational supersititious" beliefs which made them antisocial.[91] Trajan, himself, made it clear that these women were not being punished because they were Christians, but because "they form a bad precedent contrary to the real spirit of this age."[92] Trajan desired "only law and order to reign supreme" and was determined to suppress any threat to "justice and tranquility."

When the Christians were persecuted under the

---

[90]Cf. I Tim. 5:9. Cp. J.G.W. Ulhorn, *Christian Charity*, pp. 165ff.

[91]Pliny, *loc. cit.*.

[92]Pliny, *Paneg.* 34, 35 details his vengeance against the Christians. Pliny argues that only a few suffered during his reign.

empire's laws, it was only when substantial charges were brought against them before the Tribunal. Trajan, in fact, gave exceptional liberties to the Christian community—a rare experience in that age which was becoming more xenophobic and ossified.

Among the liberties and protections that Trajan favored the early Christians with was an edict which prohibited a judge from hearing any case against a Christian if the accuser was not present. Second, Trajan ruled that all civil magistrates had to enforce the laws of the land established by the Roman Senate regardless of public outcry or the blending of popular whim with personal vendetta or suspicion.[93]

Trajan's immediate successor, Hadrian the Spaniard, was even more tolerant towards Christians. He was especially concerned with the civil rights of Christian women. This was not because he was either a sexist or feminist, but because he felt that women who adopted the confession of Jesus were somehow mesmerized, confused, or "not in full control" of their faculties and reasoning abilities. Also, it must be noted, Hadrian was tolerant of the early Christians because of his own insatiable curiosity to "know all things." He sought initiation into all of the deep mysteries of religion regardless of which mystery was a part of a particular religion. He was baptized in nearly every faith, or undertook voluntary "passage" into the membership of every cult—without ever accepting any particular cult as being the absolute or having the ultimate expression of the godhead,

---

[93]Sulpic. *Sev. Chron.* II:31. Eusebius, *op. cit.* IV:26.

or even being totally in tune with the deity or deities of the "other world be it delightful as a garden, or as burdensome as a burning desert."[94] As for legislating or enforcing the current extant laws against the Christians, Hadrian demanded conclusive proof of there having been a crime committed—a truly rare objection, confirming that the "mere fact of one being a Christian" did not constitute a crime in and of itself.[95] Furthermore, in order to best meet the needs of both the state and the individual resident Christian, Hadrian ruled that a prosecutor (*delator*) of a Christian which did not make good his or her case was to be punished by the confiscation of his or her property or goods, a fine of significant proportions, and even at time with severe corporal affliction being primarily a scourging with a leather whip, a branding with hot iron, or a removal of a bodily appendage. Although legend has increased the number of atrocities allegedly committed during the reign of Hadrian, in reality we possess today only a single record of a death of any Christian: that of Pope Telesphorus.[96] Those who are accorded the rank of martyr during the reign of Hadrian have been interpolated from the Armenian *passiones* which cannot be accepted totally at face value.[97]

Executions which took place under the Emperor Pius were not as numerous, sinister, blood-thirsty or wanton as Christian apologists accuse. It is

---

[94]Tert. *Apol.* 5. Vopiscus, *Vita Saturnini* 8.

[95]Harnach, *CAL* I:317. Gibbon, I:88.

[97]Irenaeus, *Haer.* III:3.

true that more women suffered during his reign, but their martyrdoms were spearheaded by their own communities who zealously argued that the women had given up the established role of a woman, and by "having changed their sex" endangered the safety and quiet of society, threatened the children "who are confused as to what is the right way for a man and a woman to act" and by encouraging others to reevaluate their own life style and *modus operandi*. The greatest cry against Christian women during the age of Pius came when "concerned families feared the corruption of their children, trembling that the amorality [sic] of the Christian women" would "disintegrate the teachings of the parents who encouraged their sons to be soldiers and their daughters to be wives." It was as if the ancient Romans had been reading the irrational and illogical book *Child Abuse in the Classroom* by Phyllis Schlafly, or as if Anita Bryant was squeezing oranges as she paraded through the streets, encouraging emotionally charged parents who had little knowledge of the true intent of the Christians to ejaculate from trembling throats "save the children!"[98] Antonius Pius' had no true fear that the Christians would hurt the children: mentally or physically—although he was not certain of the spiritual impact the Christian women had on the "very young who eagerly seek them out". Repeatedly this age emperor has declared that he would rather "save the life of one citizen than to slay a thousand foes."[98] Thus those who were persecuted and died, died as a result of

[98]Lightfoot, *Ign.*I:481-485.

fanaticism among the populace, their sentences being confirmed by the state in the name of the emperor only when it appeared that if the executions were not completed a riot might break out and anarchy take over the already weakened system. Disorders and persecutions which Pius determinedly suppressed himself cost him his popular support and acclaim, and later pushed him into a disfavorable position in history.[99]

Even the persecutions during the reign of Marcus Aurelius are understandable when the scholar notes that the emperor permitted the execution and banishment of Christians when they went outside of the general concensus, appeared as a threat to law and order, endangered the commonweal, and encouraged open rebellion against the traditional law and order of Rome. Christian women actually suffered moreso than did Christian men who lived during the reign of Marcus Aurelius. This was because the preachings, ministration, declarations, declamations, and writings of and by Christian women encouraging the people to have hope, faith, and belief in change for the better, were in contradiction to his own philosphy and writings—a contradiction which the emperor worried would cause further physical and psychological dissettlement and quandry.[100] The Christian women's argument for hope is certainly biblical,[101] which Marcus Aurelius acknowledged in his arguement that it

[99]*Ibid.*, I:535ff.

[100]*Meditations* VI:36; cp. *ibid.* IV:27, VI:1, IX:8 and XII:5.

[101]Matt. 5:8, 48; I John 3:3.

was from a "Galilean obstinancy."[102] But since this "innovation" came out of an obscure corner of the world, a backwater region where few Romans desired to travel to and had even less knowledge about, Marcus Aurelius was convinced that it "is at best second rate, a scurrilous philosophy that has not been refined with additional thinking by great minds."

If any of the Roman emperors persecuted Christians because they believed in the message of Christ, it was Marcus Aurelius. His ultimate target was Christian women, for he feared the power of their teachings and preachings, acknowledging them to be superior priests and leaders (*episcopus*).

Marcus Aurelius saw in Christ and his promise of a "better life to come" an obstacle for the present and to the present. He believed that the Galilean's teachings were a stumbling block—if not an insurmountable wall to the revival and rise of a national religion based on Stoicism which would bring back the tarnished glory of an mighty imperial Rome. Since women were the most steadfast in maintaining the orthodoxy of the faith, he determined consciously that they were to be the primary targets for liquidation—a pogrom begun in earnest at the city of Lyons.[103]

While numerous women suffered and died at Lyons, their execution encouraged numerous others to join the Christian community. Baptisms

---

[102]*Meditations* IX:3. Ammian, XXV:4, 17. Capitolinus, *Marcus Antonius*, 13.

[102]Eusebius, *op. cit.* V:1, 17 *et supra.*.

[104]Ramsay, *ChE* 340.

into the faith of Christ were as frequent and regular as the executions—with many women being baptized in their own blood.

Determinedly the Christian women of Lyons testified to their faith. Eagerly they sought disputation with their accusers and detractors. Zealously they responded to the charges, and scoffed at the judicial requests that they abandon "the teachings and writings of the accursed sect known as Christians," affirming a desire to "give witness to the Only King Who reigns with our life blood and our love, for we will go to our marriage with the Bridegroom Who has no equal, but Who will assure us life immortal."

Such statements insulted the non-Christian citizens of Lyons, who questioned if the women of the Christian faith were advocating bigamy since many of these same women who were announcing their willingness to die and go to their bridegroom were already married to men of the city—or urging an overthrow of the government by way of "maintaining and retaining those writings" concerned with the elements of Christ's preaching and his life which were considered a threat to the social fabric of the province. But the more intensive the persecutions became, the more earnest the women were in their witnessing, proving the extent of Tertullian's often-quoted observation, "the church thrives on the blood of her martyrs."

Even though the number of martyrs was great during the time of Marcus Aurelius, and the church "gloried and grew in the wellspring of their blood," the extent has been hagiographically exaggerated. In part the exaggeration has been a result of overly ambitious apologists who attempted to instill piety, determination and perseverance in to the hearts of neophytes and confessors. But the truth of the matter concerning the number of persecutions under Marcus Aurelius is that they were small, since Marcus Aurelius was most definitely a business-minded person who preferred to fine or banish trouble-makers rather than put them to death. Dead citizens would pay no taxes which the treasury of the empire needed badly, nor could dead citizens be converted back to the old faith of the religions of imperial Rome and thus bring about the renaissance based on the glories of the past that Marcus Aurelius so dearly longed for and worked towards.[104]

Upon the death of Marcus Aurelius, the organized Christian church knew peace. The pogrom had stopped in part because of the ministration of a woman: Marcia, who was the mistress to Commodus—and even if she was not herself a Christian, was at least sympathetic to Christianity.[105]

Marcia was appalled at the number of lives lost during the reign of Marcus Aurelius. It had to be stopped, for she saw in the blood-letting of the Christians a further weakening of the strength of the empire which was polarizing towards its own destruction. The persecutions were not universally popular.[106] Thus, because of her influence and stand, those Christians who were in prison were released—including Pope Callistus.[107]

---

[105]Dio Cass. LXXII:4. Hippolyt. *Phil.* IX:12. Neumann, *RSK* I:85-86.

[106]Neumann, *ibid.*, I:283-291.

[107]Hippolyt. *loc. cit.*

During the rule of Commodus the Church grew and prospered. Marcia frequently interceded for small congregations, winning either a temporary reprieve or a lessening of their tax burden. Because of her example and enthusiasm for the "unusual sect of Christians," many ennobled and wealthy women joined the movement, completing what had become law centuries ago, allowing women control over their destiny and property, no longer chained to the chauvinistic will of an insensitive husband or father.

Many noble men joined their wives in turning to Christianity to find solace for mind and body. A good part of the court with their entire households entered *en masse* into the emerging church, attaching themselves to the eastern faith and life style.[108]

Persecutions of the early Christians did not resume until the third century. Then it broke out in fury when intimitable men felt threatened by women of quality silencing other men of quality who were not threatened by women of equality, by promising economic and personal retaliation if society as a whole did not march "against that evil regiment of women who speak out as men and for men, assuming the role of men, and becoming like men, giving up the natural order of things as if changing their own sex to that of men." Such misogynistic comments only proved the remarkable chauvinism of the day for the women were seen as a rival to the organizations run by men for men with men.[109] The male

---

[108]Neumann, *op. cit.* I:83 n.2, 84 n.2.

[109]Tert. *Apol.* 37.

members of the clergy of the Christian church attempted to meet this challenge by laying the groundwork for the unbiblical prohibition against women joining the priesthood.[110] This action cost the church many followers—many of whom sought freedom in the various "heretical sects"— such as the Gnostics.[111]

In the first half of the third century Christians made rapid advances in securing adherents and winning largesses from the faithful. Decius correctly concluded that the bishop of Rome was fastly becoming a rival emperor,[112] for Pope Fabian had substituted seven divisions of his own for the fourteen civil districts created by the emperors of the past.[113] At the same time, moreover, the wealth of the Christians had surpassed that of non-Christians—making Christians a formidable economic threat to the status quo. This not only concerned Decius, but those who assumed the imperial purple after him.[114]

Septimius Severus soon realized the sharpness of Decius' fears. In an attempt to win over the Christians, Septimius developed a cordial working condition with the Pope and even permitted a Christian slave of his household to annoint him with oil[112] even though he rejected Christianity. Septimius did not realize his folly with toying with a foreign faith that still had little interest in his

---

[110]Cyprian, *Ep.* LV:9. Cf. my *Woman as priest, bishop & laity in the early Catholic Church to 440 AD* (Mesquite, 1984).

[111]*LP* I:148. Cf. my *Woman in the early Gnostic church.*

[112]Tert. *Scap.* 4.

[113] Ruinart, *AM* 303. Tert. *de Cor..* 1.

[114]*Ibid..* Harnack, *MC* 117.

empire or the goals of the non-Christians until he was faced with mutiny among his troops. His army was increasingly composed of Christians who refused to fight. Such a concern for pacificism was paramount among Perpetua and her companions who are on record as having suffered for the crimes of "bribing the soldiers (*constituerunt praemio uti paucis horis emissi meliorem...*).[115]

Septimius Severus died at York on 4 February 211 before he accomplished his goal of reuniting the empire. The Church openly celebrated his death for Septimius was succeed by a series of worthless sons who did little in the area of governing and refused to concern themselves with the growing power of popes which they found "amusing. They never realized the threat the church was posing in its grasp to assume control over the minds and bodies of all Romans so that literature, thought, science would be limited rigidly to its increasing staid and ossified credo, ending the dignity of humankind and the glory of inquiry and the pursuit of the excellence of knowledge. During this period of time the church experienced a relative calm within and without. This calm lasted until the murder of Alexander Severus and his mother who were staying at Mainz. Their murder brought a renewed interest in curtailing the misused freedom of the Christians.

In many ways the renewed persecutions of the Christians following the assassination of Alexander Severus and his mother at Mainze was a popular reaction against the emperor and his

---

[115]*Passio Sanctarum Perpetuae et Felicitatis,* as cited. See also my commentary as cited.

parent, for the common concensus was that Alexander's mother had too much power and influence over the emperor, having been guided to assert herself by select Christian women. This of course, was untrue, for historically women in the age of the empire were not only free but encouraged to take a political and social stand, in many cases governing their houses and becoming active in civic affairs, while Christian women were becoming more restricted by the gynophobia of men. But, regardless, women were seen as detriments to law and order, and as sirens who could confuse capable men dedicated to the strong restoration of the empire and imperial majesty.[116]

When Decius assumed the reigns of the entire empire, his bitterness towards the Christians was realized in raw confrontations. The emperor was embittered beyond any expectation. Decius saw the Christians as a "collection of self-indulgent effeminate men, painted women, and ambitious clergy" whose first love was themself and their personal aggrandizement, with their last concern being the empire, the safety of the people, or the increased prosperity of the realm.[117] To "end this curse" Decius had no hesitation to send Christians to their death, although the majority who suffered under him during his reign were given long prison terms to be served under the most intolerable conditions.

250 CE was the most critical year for the Christians under Decius short reign. Pope Fabian who was becoming increasingly an annoying and

---

[116]Eusebius, *HE* VI:28.

[117]Cyprian, *de Lapsis* 5.

troublesome thorn in the flesh of Decius was executed. The pontiff's departure from this world quickly opened the gates to death for numerous other Christians, so devastating the Christian clergy and community that not only was there no successor chosen to fill the throne of Peter for the next fourteen months,[118] but women stopped preaching so as not to attrack the attention of loyal imperial troops who were opposed to Christianity and its spread. Their self-imposed silence gave the men of the church an opportunity to come out against women as priests and preachers with the lame argument that their duty was to be in the home, instructing their children, and honoring their husbands.

Even though a few strong hearted women objected and urged the women clergy of the church to continue to preach, admonishing them by saying, "if you do not use your power God granted you, truly you will lose it now and for future generations," women gave up their mission for the sake of security at home. Few chose to remember the determination of Phoebe or Prisca or any of the other priests of Rome Paul saluted in his epistle to the churches of Rome.

The number of women who were executed rose dramatically in spite of their acceptance of public silence. The greatest number of Christian martyred women suffered in Africa where Christianity had an uniquely strong hold, in part because of the economic conditions, in part because the transitory animistic religions of North Africa offered little in the way of future eschatological pro-

[118]*LP* I:148. Cf. my *Woman under Decius* (Toronto, 1981).

mise, and in part because of the trade routes which crossed bringing to the entrepots the best of all theological offerings. When the pogorm was pushed by the arrival of imperial troops it was the women who stood fast for the faith of Christ. More women suffered death in the name of Christianity than did men, and more men apostacized the Christian faith than did women, leaving the women as victims to butcherous blood baths that flowed from arenas into the streets, up hills, on roof tops, in gulleys, and within barracks where women were taken to be raped serially by troops and gladiators. Others, especially the men who died, like Lucian and his companions, were condemned to a slow death—dying together in a prison from hunger and thirst.[119]

The deaths of the women in North Africa, coupled with the legendary zeal with which men encouraged them to "win the crown of martyrdom" spurred an increase in conversions, and in the growing number of confessors who raced "up to the tribunal and declare[d]" that t. , were Christians eager to die for their faith.[120] This strange interest in dying, and the zealous race towards death by public confrontation with Roman officials was especially keen in Egypt where the greatest number of martyrs were counted during the reign of Decius and his successors.

Respite from the persecutions and blood baths was not to be had even when the soldier Diocletian ascended the imperial throne. After he put on the purple, the situation became increasingly

[119]Cyprian, *de Lap.* 7, 8, 9, 13, 24f. Cf. his *Epp.* 6, 9, 11, 14, 22, 24, 38, 40f. Cf. my *Woman and Cyprian in the Early Church* (Boston, 1979).

[120]Eusebius, *ibid.* VII:11

Diocletian
(Caesar 284-305 CE)
His reforms were meant to restore the stability of the empire after the chaotic third century. In an effort to meet this goal he had Christians arrested, tortured, and in some cases put to death on the charge of treason, or being "a dissettling influence." [Culver Pictures.]

tense and critical. Victim after victim fell to the rapacious roar of malignant multitudes.[121] Women, again were singled out: forced to sacrifice to the old gods of the decaying empire, or to be put to death being found guilty of incendiarism, atheism, or treason.[122]

Diocletian's retirement on 1 May 305 further intensified the persecutions. At Caesarea 97 men, women and children were blinded in one eye, had their left foot disabled by hot irons, and were forced to journey on foot to the mines of Phaeno.[123] Within months the flames of persecution grew red hot, and by the autumn of 308 a new reign of terror commenced, primarily seeking out women who were "feared as the corruptors of men and children." Strict censorship was enforced, and those who were suspect were arrested without warrant or charge.

It was not until 30 April 311 that an edict of toleration was issued *ut denuo sint Christiani.* Then this edict was issued only because Galerius was on his death-bed and "wished to have himself protected from all gods." He confessed that his action occured because he had failed to induce his victims to "display reverence for the [Roman] gods" when "those accursed women stood fast and urged their compatriots to hold to the faith" of the Nazarene. Since he could not whip the

---

[121]*Ibid.* VIII (4) 2; cf. *ibid.* VIII:1, (6) 6. The women who did apostatize their faith held on to the "pagan" belief even after Christianity was legalized for fear of renewed persecutions. See Gelzer, *Die Anfange...*; cf. my *Woman and the Persecutions in North Africa* (Toronto, 1981), and my *Execution of the Lady Crispina* (Mesquite, 1980).

[122]*Passio Felcis*, as cited.

[123]Eusebius, *MP* 8.

Christians, and was afraid of his own mortality, he decided on the edict of toleration in expectation and anticipation that the Christians would "pray to their god for our recovery." He died five days later.[124]

---

[124]*Ibid.* VIII:17. Cf. Broglie, *L'eglise et l'empire* I:207. Eusebius gives the final account in *HE* IX (1) 4: "everywhere the faithful returned to commence building and rebuilding churches...."

The Role of Martyrdom:
It's Psychological Impact
on the Christian Church

Women were the first to accept the Christian message: ranging from Mary the mother of Jesus, who according to the writings of the Christians, received the annunciation of her parthenogenetic conception, to the other Mary who was the first to see at least the image of Jesus after his alleged resurrection. Women were also in the forefront of those who testified to the message of Jesus, spanning the initial input of the mother of Jesus in the upper room in Jerusalem when allegedly the deity descended into the midst of the apostles of Jesus and gave them the power to speak "in tongues", to the first priests of this new cult from the Middle East: Prisca, Phoebe, and other women.

At the same time it was women who were among the first to be singled out and attacked because they adhered to the message of the man from Galilee (although, according to the Christian writings, a young Greek Jew by the name of Stephen was the first to die in witnessing the message at the hands of Saul of Tarsus). Their convictions and beliefs that they would be with this Jesus in an afterlife gave the women who delighted in calling themselves Christians a special marking which, even according to non-Christian records, gave them a special "radiance" and the ability to sing psalms as they were being led and/or sent to their deaths, many of which were cruelly prolonged and inhumane by any standard, being not only traditional tortures. For, whereas men were either generally consigned to the arena to face gladiators, were crucified, decapitated (the penalty suffered by Basilides), or forced to fight wild animals on as near an equal footing as was conceived, women were treated more shabbily, being sewn into the hides of animals and then put into arenas to be attacked and eaten by other animals, hung from posts (as was the fate of Blandina), exposed to starved wild beasts after being flagellated, scourged, speared, suffered hooks and daggars, had their breasts cut off (as happened to St Barbara), were immersed or covered with boiling pitch (as occurred in the execution of Potamiaena), made into living candles (as used in the gardens of Nero), or were put into brothels to be raped repeatedly by legions of men, and the like.[126]

If the contemporary historian and scholarly only had the hortatory hagiographic accounts of the Christian apologists, it would be easy to write off these records as pious propaganda. However, since the contemporary non-Christian Romans also wrote on the plight and end of many martyrs of the Christian community, it is not possible to do other than acknowledge the depth of the conviction of those who chose to die for what they believed in fervently. For many of these early Christians, death was not only a release from the trials and tribulations of earthly existence which was stark, staid, ossified, almost Reaganesque in

---

[125]Adolf Harnack, "Die Akten des Krapus, des Papulus und der Agathonike," in *Texte und Untersuchungen zur Geschichte der altchristlichen Literatur* 3.3-4 (1888) p. 440-454. Eusebius, *HE* VI:5, 4; and my various translations of martyrdoms as cited above.

its disinterest in the lot of the poor and the unlettered, but too, death was looked forward to as a ticket into a better world than the one on earth; an opportunity to never again hunger, thirst, be lonely, discounted, ignored, unwanted, and unloved. These early Christians sought to be like sheep following the "good shepherd," who would protect them from all manner of dissettlement, and to be "first where they had been last." It is true, in the reading of some of the *passiones*, some of the martyrs believed that they would gain greater recognition in death from their society than they had merited while alive, and this can be analyzed appropriately as an expression of ego and individual need even if necromanic. Then too, others delighted in goading the authority of the state, or in playing censor, judge, or determiner over the destiny of those who did not, would not, or could not concur with their narrow and stagnantly limiting program for human existence. It was truly proto-Falwellian and rankly undemocratic, being destructive to individual expression refining its magnificence and splendor in a plethora of diversity. But, all things considered, one must accord these early Christians with a special courage to accept a fate few would desire, embrace or forgive. This is what made them unique and memorable.

INDEX